A COMPLETE PROPERTY BUYER'S GUIDE 2005/06
BY DOMINIC WHITING

ORDER ONLINE AT

WWW.BUYINGINTURKEY.INFO

apogee *publishing*

Buying in Turkey 2005/06

BY DOMINIC WHITING www.buyinginturkey.info

BY DOMINIC WHITING
www.buyinginturkey.info
First edition 2005/06

Additional Research: Özge Dursun **Editorial Advisor:** Ayşe Özcan
Managing Editor & Publisher: Dominic Whiting
Art Director: Gary Ottewill **Design:** Editorial Design Ltd
Photography: Dominic Whiting **Additional Photography:** Tim Goodman
Sales Directors: Daniel Fisher & Luke Hope **Sales Assistant:** Gaby Mack
Sales & Publishing Representative (Turkey): Özge Dursun **Sales Assistant (Turkey):** Fatoş Sevimli
Cover Image: Dominic Whiting/hanelhouses.com **Title/Credit Page Image:** Dominic Whiting/tandemvillas.com

Published by Apogee Publishing, 70 Mornington Street, London, NW1 7QE, UK.
info@apogee-publishing.com   ©Apogee Publishing Ltd. 2005.
Every effort has been made to ensure that the facts in this guide are accurate at the time of going to press. However, the author and
publisher cannot accept responsibility for any loss, injury or inconvenience resulting from the use of this book. Seek the necessary
professional advice before proceeding with any property transaction. Printed in Turkey by Doğan Ofset A.S. www.doganofset.com

apogee *publishing*

Contents

Turkey is the Mediterranean's most exciting emerging property market. So whether you're looking for a dream villa, a retirement home in the sun or an investment property, this guide will help you do it. Discover the country, learn about the practicalities of life and find out about the most popular places to buy. There's also a Directory of useful contacts and websites. Happy property hunting!

Country Background

The Aegean

West Mediterranean

Buying Property

Living in Turkey

East Mediterranean

Istanbul & Information

PropertyMap

Turkey's most popular places to buy, covered in this guide, are mainly along the Aegean and Mediterranean coasts

AYVALIK
Greek houses for renovation in the old town
page 83

ÇEŞME
Popular with Turks, largely unknown to foreign buyers
page 84

ALTINKUM
Budget property in a popular package destination
page 87

BODRUM
A cosmopolitan resort, with a wide choice of property
page 89-90

FETHIYE
Villas, apartments... with plenty to see and do
page 98-101

BLACK SEA

●ISTANBUL

●ANKARA

●Ayvalık

TURKEY

●Çeşme
●Kuşadası
●Altınkum
●Bodrum
●Cappadocia
Datça● ●Marmaris Antalya
Dalaman●●Fethiye ● ●Side
Kalkan● ● ●Alanya
Kaş Kemer

MEDITERRANEAN SEA

BUYING IN
TURKEY

KALKAN
Villas with spectacular views
page 104-105

SIDE
Fine beaches and ancient ruins
page 114

ALANYA
Popular with investment buyers
page 117

CAPPADOCIA
Historic cave and stone houses
page 121

ISTANBUL
Inner-city and suburban living
page 124-125

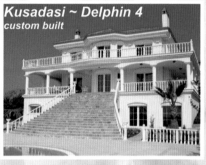

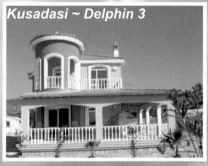

Country Background

History

Istanbul's Sultanahmet Mosque is one of the country's many architectural treasures

At a crossroads of civilisations, Turkey has a fascinating history stretching from Neolithic times to the modern republic of today

TURKEY AT A GLANCE
Area: 770,760 sq km
(x3 larger than the UK)
Population: 70 million
Official Language: Turkish
Capital City: Ankara
Religion: 99% Muslim

AT THE EASTERN END OF THE MEDITERRANEAN, located between Europe, Asia and the Middle East, Turkey has enjoyed an extremely long and colourful past. Some of the earliest human settlements grew up within the country over 10,000 years ago. At Çatal Höyük, near the city of Konya, archaeologists have unearthed a Neolithic town – some of the oldest known real estate in the world. Since then, Anatolia – as the landmass forming the country is called – has been a bridge, across which successive tides of civilization have swept. The mysterious Hittites, the ancient Greeks, the Persians, the Romans and their successors, the Byzantines, all held sway over what is now Turkey. Each people left a wealth of archaeological and architectural treasures scattered across the country. The awe-inspiring

Byzantine cathedral of Haghia Sophia, the well-preserved Roman theatre at Aspendos, the Library of Celsus at Ephesus and the Hittite city of Hattuşaş, to name but a few. The Turkish countryside is also littered with hundreds of smaller historic sites too. In fact, it is often said that Turkey has more ancient Greek remains than Greece; more Roman ruins than Italy, making it a paradise for amateur archaeologists and sightseers.

In 1453, Byzantine Constantinople, once the wealthiest city in all of Christendom, fell to the Turkish army of Mehmet the Conqueror. As the new Ottoman capital of Istanbul, the city was home to the opulent court of the sultans, with its mysterious harem, for over 400 years. At the heart of a mighty empire, stretching at its peak from the Persian Gulf to North Africa, from the Crimea south to Arabia, the city was graced with mosques, palaces and castles, many of which are still standing today. Despite its immense size and wealth, the Ottoman Empire suffered a slow, inexorable decline, which culminated in its ignoble defeat in the First World War.

The Turkish Republic was established in 1923 following a bitterly fought war between invading Greek forces and Turkish nationalists led by Mustafa Kemal. As the country's first president, Mustafa Kemal, who became known as Atatürk, or "Father of the Turks", began a series of ambitious reforms aimed at rebuilding the country from the ashes of the Ottoman Empire and turning it into a modern, western-looking country (see below).

RECOMMENDED READS
A Traveller's History of Turkey
Richard Stoneman
Turkey: A Short History
Roderic Davidson

ORDER ONLINE AT
www.buyinginturkey.info

Atatürk
Father of the Turks

Standing in town squares; watching as you arrive at the airport or visit the post office; even nestling in your wallet, the country's first president and national hero, Atatürk, is everywhere in Turkey. Born in 1881 in the Aegean town of Salonika – in present-day Greece – Atatürk became an officer in the Ottoman army, distinguishing himself in the bloody First World War battles at Gallipoli. Decorated and promoted, Atatürk used his position to organise a nationalist resistance movement to fight invading Greek forces and eventually establish a democratic government in the new capital, Ankara.

But Atatürk didn't stop there, as he wanted to turn the new Turkey into a modern, European country. Writing a new constitution; setting-up Parliament; getting rid of the last Sultan; giving women the vote; replacing Arabic with the Latin alphabet; even banning the traditional Ottoman hat, the fez; he achieved a lot in only 15 years. But many see Turkey's accession to the EU as the ultimate achievement of Atatürk's dreams.

Partial to a drop of the Turkish national drink, rakı, Ataturk died of cirrhosis of the liver in 1938. If you're in the country on 10 November, a minute silence is still observed for the "Father of the Turks".

Climate&Landscape

Taking off from one of the country's Mediterranean beaches.

From the olive groves of the Mediterranean to the barren mountains of the east, Turkey has an extremely varied landscape.

The snowy summit of Mount Ararat, Turkey's highest mountain.

TURKEY'S CLIMATE AND TOPOGRAPHY – like it's history-are amazingly diverse. Uniquely, the country straddles two continents, with the narrow straits of the Bosphorus and the Dardanelles dividing Europe from Asia. Mountains cover much of the country, with the highest peak, Mt Ararat, rising to 5,166 metres in the east. Mountain ranges flank the Mediterranean, Aegean and Black Sea coasts, enclosing a high plateau in the center of the country. Winters are severe across this central region, as well as in the east, with temperatures dropping to a finger-numbing -30C in some areas. With mountains and lots of snow, it is not surprising that there are some ski resorts open during the winter months.

At the opposite end of the temperature gauge, the country's south-east, near the Syrian border, is sweltering hot in summer with highs of over 40C. Along the Aegean and Mediterranean coasts, where the tourist industry and foreign property market are concentrated, the climate is far more pleasant, with mild winters and hot, sunny weather during the summer. Temperatures climb into the high 30Cs in July, but there are often cooling sea breezes near the coast. Most rain falls during the winter months, although periods of crisp, sunny weather are common in winter too. Even along the southern coast winter temperatures can be surprisingly cold.

BODRUM AVERAGE MONTHLY TEMP °C

LANDSCAPE

Large areas of the Turkish countryside are very unspoilt. Pine-forested mountains cover much of the Aegean and Mediterranean regions, with olive groves, citrus orchards and fields of vegetables, tobacco and cotton where the land is flatter.

The country's best beaches are dotted along the Mediterranean coast, roughly from Dalyan to Alanya. Further north, the coastline between Marmaris and Bodrum has a series of deep bays and peninsulars. The area is extremely beautiful and well-suited for sailing. The Aegean coast has some good streches of beach, notably at Altınkum and Çeşme, although being further north the season is slightly shorter.

AVERAGE MONTHLY
RAINFALL

BODRUM AVERAGE MONTHLY RAINFALL CM

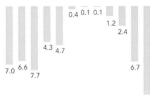

The Black Sea coast, Turkey's wettest region, is backed by thickly forested mountains, with dairy farms, tea-plantations and hazelnut orchards on the lower slopes. The landscape of Central Anatolia is made up of rolling fields of wheat and grazing land. The strangely eroded landscape and fascinating historical sites of Cappadocia, to the south east of the capital Ankara, attract tourists and a small but growing number of home buyers.

Turkey is self-sufficient in most agricultural produce, exporting fruit, vegetables, dairy products and meat to the EU and the Middle East. A visit to any local Turkish market will give you an idea of the amazing wealth and quality of what's grown in the country. Perhaps best known for its Mediterranean crops, such as olives, tomatoes, peaches, apricots, melons and citrus, temperate fruit like apples, pears, plums and cherries are also available on a seasonal basis. Bananas are even grown along the sub-tropical southern coast near Alanya.

Fishing is an important industry along the 8,000 km coast, although it has been eclipsed by tourism particularly along the Aegean and Mediterranean coasts. Away from towns and cities most people still earn their living from farming and the pace of life in rural areas is very slow.

The "Fairy Chimneys" of Cappdocia in Central Turkey.

Culture&Religion

Turkey has a young, dynamic population, most of whom live in rapidly growing cities like Ankara, Istanbul and Izmir

Turkish people are generally far more moderate in their religious beliefs than their neighbours in the Middle East

MODERN TURKS ARE THE DESCENDENTS of nomadic tribes who migrated from Central Asia with their flocks. The country also has significant minority groups, such as Kurds, Arabs and Laz.

Turkey's national religion is Islam, but the country is a secular state with religious affairs and government kept firmly apart. Turkish people are generally far more moderate in their religious beliefs than their neighbours in the Middle East. This is particularly the case in the main cities and the coastal resorts. More conservative attitudes tend to be found in the less developed and eastern parts of the country. Women in these areas typically choose to cover their heads with a headscarf, although few veil themselves completely.

In the main cities and resort areas most Turkish women dress in Western-style clothes. But outside these areas, where more traditional attitudes prevail, visitors should dress more modestly to avoid attracting unwanted attention or causing offence.

Remember not to wear shorts or short sleeves when visiting a mosque, and women will need to put on a headscarf too. Alcohol is widely available in bars, restaurants and shops, and many Turkish people enjoy a drink.

The main religious holidays of the Islamic calendar, such as Ramazan, are widely observed in Turkey. Banks, government offices and many businesses are closed, and Turkish people traditionally visit their family and relatives.

Turkey has a young and rapidly growing population with 50% of its people under 25 years old. In the last 40 years there has been a huge movement of people from the countryside to towns and cities like Ankara and Istanbul. Over 60% of the population now live in urban areas, although their connection with family and friends still living in the countryside often remains strong.

RECOMMENDED READS
Culture Shock! Turkey
Arin Bayraktroglu

ORDER ONLINE AT
www.buyinginturkey.info

European attitudes are common in the resorts and the main cities where most foreigners buy property.

Politics

Turkey is a secular democracy, with the current government committed to carrying out the reforms necessary to start the EU entry process

TURKEY WAS RULED AS A SINGLE-PARTY STATE until 1950, when an experiment with multi-party politics led to victory for the opposition Democratic Party. Since then, Turkish political parties have multiplied, but democracy has been interrupted by periods of political instability. There have also been times of political conflict, notably during the 1970s, between extremists of the right and left. The military, as self-proclaimed guardians of the secular ideals of the country's founder, Atatürk, have played an important role in politics. *Coups* in 1960, 1971 and 1980, removed civilian governments and established martial law, although power was eventually returned to the politicians each time. More recently, the military stepped into the political arena in 1997, helping to unseat the pro-Islamic government of Necmettin Erbakan. Despite these interventions, the army is the most widely trusted and popular state institution.

THE POLITICAL SYSTEM

The Turkish Republic has a secular, pluralist parliamentary system. Legislative power rests with the National Assembly or *Meclis* in Ankara, with 550 deputies elected every 5 years by a system of proportional representation. A 10% electoral threshold was recently introduced to limit the number of smaller political parties in the Parliament. The nation is governed by a Council of Ministers headed by the Prime Minister, presently Tayyip Erdoğan of the AK Party. The head of state is the president, currently Ahmet Necdet, who is elected every 7 years by parliament and presides over the powerful National Security Council, made up of top members of the government and armed forces.

Modern Turkish politics has been plagued by factionalism, with weak coalition governments contributing to a series of economic crises and poor overall performance. This political instability came to an end in 2002, when the AK Party was elected with over 30% of the popular vote and a large majority in parliament. Despite concerns among secular Turks and the military about the party's mildly Islamic credentials, the government of Recep Tayyip Erdoğan has used its parliamentary majority to push through a series of difficult economic and social reforms aimed at stabilizing the economy and bringing the country into line to start EU accession negotiations. Among these reforms was a liberalisation of the laws governing foreign property buyers, although parts of this legislation were ruled unconstitutional in March, 2005 by the Turkish Supreme Court, and new legislation is currently being drafted (see page 37).

The government has also won praise for its willingness to tackle sensitive issues, such as minority rights and the future of Cyprus, where 30,000 Turkish troops remain in the divided north of the island.

RECOMMENDED READS

Turkey Unveiled
Nicole and Hugh Pope

ORDER ONLINE AT
www.buyinginturkey.info

Turkey and the EU

Turkey became an associate member of what was then the European Economic Community in 1963, although it didn't formally apply for full membership until 1987. Since then, many Turks have been frustrated by their apparent lack of progress, with Brussels refusing to set a date for the start of entry negotiations until Turkey had met certain conditions. Many of the recent reforms introduced by the AK party government were aimed at meeting these targets, opening the way for a decision by the EU to start formal negotiations in October 2005. However, experts acknowledge that it will be at least 10 years, possibly as long as 15 or even 20, before Turkey is finally allowed to join. Despite such slow progress, opinion polls show that over 70% of Turks are in favour of EU membership, although the country still has to introduce many painful reforms in order to qualify. It also has to overcome considerable public opposition from within member states such as Austria and France.

The**Economy**

Turkey's private sector is leading the country out of one of its worst recessions.

Despite a turbulent past, the Turkish economy is performing well
though significant challenges still lie ahead

AT A GLANCE
GDP: $509 Billion
GDP (per capita): $7,350
GDP Growth rate: 7.2% (2004)
Inflation: 9%
Currency: New Turkish Lira

TURKEY HAS A VERY DYNAMIC ECONOMY with a vigorous and rapidly growing private sector. However, the state maintains an important role in many areas of the economy, such as heavy industry, banking, transport, and communication. Privatisation, although a priority of several consecutive governments, has been slow. Inefficient and badly managed public firms still dominate large parts of the economy and remain a major drain on the national purse.

The country's most important industries are textiles and clothing, employing between them over 35% of the workforce. These sectors also produce the country's main exports, although other manufacturing industries, such as car making and electronics, are of growing significance. Low labour rates and proximity to markets in Europe and the Middle East have encouraged the growth of these manufacturing industries. Agriculture remains an important economic activity, employing around 40% of the country's labour force. Despite widespread mechanisation and large-scale irrigation projects, traditional farming methods and low production predominate in many areas.

Underlying structural problems within the economy, coupled with

Expert View
The Turkish Economy

How has Turkey's economy improved in recent years?
After the dramatic events of February 2001 when the currency devalued and a financial crisis sent many banks and firms into bankruptcy, an austerity program, designed with the IMF, was implemented. Over the last 3 years, Turkey has successfully introduced a series of structural reforms as part of this program, and IMF involvement has been renewed for another 3 years. Public finances were restructured, the banking sector was reformed and the privatisation process was re-started. However, more importantly, the EU gave Turkey a date (October 3rd, 2005) to start accession talks.

Turkey achieved GNP growth after 2002, reaching 9.9% in 2004. Inflation, which floated between 40% and 150%, was curbed to single digits (9.32%) by the end of 2004. As both macro-economic conditions and political outlook have improved, so stability of the country's financial markets has also been achieved.

How has the prospect of EU membership helped the economic situation?
EU membership was the most significant factor in the recent surge in asset prices, including Turkish property, as the long feared risk of political and administrative instability has been replaced by the prospect of EU convergence. The convergence

Saruhan Doğan is Senior Vice President of the Treasury Research and Sales Department at Finansbank. www.finansbank.com.tr

"Careful assessment of the specific property is key to making a value creating decision"

process has attracted European investors, but they should remain conscious of the risks in the Turkish market.

What is the outlook for the Turkish economy?
The performance of the economy depends critically on two interrelated issues: commitment to continuing economic and political reform and further improving relationships with the EU. The AK Party government has proved so far that the EU membership process is its main priority and we believe that Turkish assets will appreciate further after talks start on October 3rd. The growth rate of GNP, which has been volatile throughout the last two decades, is expected to stabilize and sustainable growth of around 5% will be achieved.

Do you recommend foreign investors buy property in Turkey?
We do recommend the purchase of real estate. However, a careful assessment of the specific property is key to making a value creating decision. Coastal areas where tourism is developing quickly and developing industrial cities, such as Istanbul, where housing is scarce are the two main areas that we believe property will appreciate in value in the years to come.

The local economy along the south coast – the main area for foreign property buyers – is now dominated by tourism

political mismanagement and global events, caused a series of economic crises during the 1990s. These culminated in a catastrophic devaluation in 2001, when the Turkish Lira lost 40% of its value. Thousands lost their jobs, while the country's GDP plummeted by over 7%.

An IMF-sponsored recovery plan introduced by the government of Bülent Ecevit helped stabilise the situation, although it was left to the AK Party government, elected in 2002, to guide the Turkish economy out of its worst recession since the Second World War. Fiscal belt tightening and economic reform have succeeded in cutting the government deficit. Inflation has been brought down from a galloping 70% to 11.4% in 2004. Industrial production in the third quarter of last year was up 6.8% compared to 2003 and GDP grew by 4.5 %.

Much needed reforms within the banking industry have boosted investor confidence and the improving economic climate have resulted in growing foreign investment.

Despite these dramatic improvements there remain considerable economic challenges ahead, such as improving the country's tax base, reducing unemployment and dealing with inefficient state owned businesses. However, the present government, enjoying strong popular support and IMF backing, maintains its commitment to tackling these problems in order to stay on track for eventual EU membership.

Traditionally an agricultural region, raising citrus crops and vegetables for the domestic market and export, the local economy along the south coast – the main area for foreign property buyers - is now dominated by tourism. Fishing remains an important economic activity in some areas, while forestry and animal husbandry are significant in the coastal mountains.

The**Property**Market

With its picturesque harbour and castle, Bodrum is one of the country's most popular places to buy.

Turkish property is enjoying unprecedented interest from foreign buyers due to its affordability and the prospect of EU membership

Sun, sand and sea: the same things that attract tourists are now encouraging property buyers.

A WELL–ESTABLISHED PACKAGE DESTINATION visited by millions of British and European tourists each year, Turkey has only recently emerged as a popular place to buy property. All the ingredients that made the country such a good holiday spot – a warm Mediterranean climate, lovely scenery, friendly people and excellent value for money – are now fuelling an unprecedented level of interest in the country from foreign buyers. Current prices are far lower than other, more established, property markets, such as Spain and Italy. The prospect of EU membership in the not-too-distant future also promises excellent potential for capital growth as Turkish property prices are expected to climb to levels found elsewhere in the Mediterranean.

Outside interest in Turkish property has also been encourage by a liberalisation of the laws governing foreign buyers in 2003. These changes opened up rural areas to overseas buyers and created a more investor friendly environment.

Despite all the excitement, the Turkish market is still comparatively small by international standards- the $1.34 billion invested in Turkish property by foreigners in 2004 compares with

TURKEY'S HOTTEST
PROPERTY SPOTS

Kuşadası: A large package resort town with marina and easy access to Ephesus, Turkey's most impressive archaeological site, as well as Izmir airport.

Altınkum: A rapidly growing resort popular with British and Turkish tourists for its sandy beach. Close to Bodrum airport.

Bodrum: The country's most sophisticated resort, with interesting sights, good shopping and excellent nightlife. Beyond the main town are a string of very different, smaller resorts.

Çalış: Fethiye's nearest beach resort is attracting British buyers in droves thanks to some very affordable property and a long stretch of seashore.

Hisarönü & Ovacik: Set in lovely mountain scenery with the Ölüdeniz lagoon nearby, these two resorts near Fethiye are hugely popular with buyers – particularly from Britain. However prices have risen dramatically in recent years.

Kalkan: An attractive, friendly resort with plenty to do in the surrounding area. The town has grown explosively in recent years.

Side: Sandy beaches and Roman remains have made Side a popular resort. Now the area boasts villa and apartment complexes.

Alanya: A large seaside town with good beaches, entertainment and services. Wide choice of apartments and a large expatriate community.

over $9 billion in Spain. It is also heavily concentrated along the Aegean and Mediterranean coasts, and particularly the stretch between the resort of Kuşadası in the north and Alanya in the east. It will be no surprise that this area contains most of the country's main holiday resorts, as well as some of the most beautiful scenery and the best beaches.

Tourist development and building, particularly over the last 15 years, have transformed quaint little fishing towns like Bodrum, Marmaris and Alanya into large resorts boasting modern leisure facilities, restaurants and nightlife, as well as efficient hospitals and well-stocked supermarkets. Large-scale projects, such as the golf courses around Belek, east of Antalya, and modern marinas in resorts such as Marmaris, Göcek and Fethiye have added to the appeal for many investors and buyers. Those seeking a quiet Mediterranean hideaway may be disappointed by this transformation, but once away from the main towns, rural life continues much as it always has done.

The most popular spots for foreign property buyers and investors are Kuşadası, Altınkum, the Bodrum Peninsular, Marmaris, the Fethiye area, including the resorts of Çalış, Hisarönü and Ovacik, and Kalkan. In these areas, British buyers are generally in the majority, with German, Dutch and Scandinavians also buying in increasing numbers. Further east, Side and Alanya are also very popular, particularly with buyers from Scandinavia, Ireland and the UK. Property in Istanbul and Cappadocia in Central Anatolia is also attracting outside interest, though far less than in the coastal areas.

Most property in the coastal areas is bought for use as holiday homes, although a small but growing number of people are choosing to relocate permanently to Turkey, tempted by the quality of life and low cost of living. Many holiday homes are rented out when not in use, but investors are also increasingly looking to Turkish property to provide a buy-to-let income, as well as capital growth.

The Mediterranean and Aegean resorts are also popular with Turkish second-home buyers, with domestic demand set to increase as stable economic conditions and the introduction of a mortgage system make owning a holiday home possible for more middle-class families. Generally speaking, lower budgets mean that Turkish buyers tend to opt for certain property types, which are less popular with overseas buyers. This has caused a dual market to develop in many areas, with some construction companies targeting the foreign market by building larger, more expensive villas or apartments with better fixtures and fittings; while others build and sell almost exclusively to Turks.

Previously, many foreigners chose to buy land and have properties built themselves. This was largely due to the low-cost of building and a shortage of suitable properties, with most constructed according to local budgets and tastes. The scarcity of old buildings suitable for renovation was also a contributing factor. More recently, however, there has been a dramatic improvement in the quality of

Expert View
Property

What is encouraging foreign interest in Turkish residential property?
The country's location close to Europe and its pleasant Mediterranean climate are major draws for foreign buyers, as are the country's reasonable property prices. The recent economic and political stability in the country is also an important factor.

Is Turkish property a good investment?
Yes, as the prices of residential property are very reasonable at the moment compare to other European markets. There is also the potential for significant capital growth in the coming years, as Turkey begins accession talks with the EU and the infrastructure improves as a result of state and private investment.

What are the best areas for foreigners to buy?
The south and west coasts of Turkey are the most attractive for foreign buyers. These areas have the best scenery and also the best facilities for holidaymakers. The main areas of demand are the Aegean coast from Kuşadasi to Bodrum and on to Marmaris and Dalaman/Fethiye. The so-called Turkish Riviera from Kemer to Antalya and Alanya is also popular. All these coastal areas have a warm, dry climate and have traditionally been the main tourist destinations.

Tevfik Türel: "We hope that a mortgage system will be operational in 2006"

"Prices of residential property are very reasonable compared to Europe"

When will Turkey develop a mortgage system?
The foundations for a mortgage system will be in place next year, when the government is scheduled to pass the necessary legislation. Once the law is issued, I believe there will be mortgage packages available within 6 months. So we hope that in the 3rd quarter of 2006 a mortgage system will be fully operational in Turkey.

Are there any recommendations you have for foreign buyers?
Title is the magic word in Turkey. Everything revolves around the title of a property, so clarity is very important for buyers in order to protect their investment. Careful research is needed, but there are also products such as title insurance and title guarantees, that can help investors have piece of mind and security. The location of a property should also be investigated well. Foreigners, for example, are not permitted to buy near restricted military zones.

Tevfik Türel is Senior Vice President and Director of Eurasia and Middle East Operations for Stewart International, a global real estate information and transaction management company. www.stewart.com

27

Fethiye has a variety of property, from town center apartments to villas.

TURKEY'S EMERGING PROPERTY SPOTS

Çeşme: Largely ignored by foreign buyers, this resort is very popular with Turks and has good beaches, world-class windsurfing and some attractive property.

Gumuşluk: A small village on the Bodrum peninsular which has some very keenly priced new developments.

Dalaman: state-sponsored infrastructural and tourism projects have caused intense interest from developers and buyers in this area.

Datça: A quiet harbour town which has good beaches. Previously quite isolated, the road from Marmaris has now been improved.

properties being built by Turkish developers. Buying new builds and off-plan has become very popular, with many builders now offering units for sale on complexes with facilities like swimming pools, gyms and cafes. Some even offer guaranteed rental income, thanks to agreements with package holiday operators.

WHERE TO BUY

The Aegean resort of Çeşme and the coastline to the north have largely been the preserve of Turkish buyers. Within commuting distance of Izmir, the country's third largest city, Çeşme is a popular weekend destination, which enjoys a buoyant property market driven by local, rather than foreign, demand. Although many properties in the area still offer excellent value for money, prices in the most desirable locations have sky-rocketed.

Kuşadasi is a sprawling, rapidly growing resort town close to the fascinating Roman city of Ephesus, Turkey's most famous archaeological attraction. Similarly, Altınkum has a good beach, plenty of activities and interesting archaeological sites nearby. Both resorts have experienced massive development in recent years and are particularly popular with buyers looking for the most affordable property, be it apartments or cheap villas.

The Bodrum Peninsular is a diverse area with something to suit all tastes and budgets. Its popularity with domestic and expatriate Turkish buyers, many of them extremely wealthy, has pushed prices up. But consequently, the area has a wide choice of properties at all levels of the market, as well as excellent leisure facilities, services and amenities.

Further south, the large town and package resort of Marmaris boasts a marina and a sandy beach at Içmeler. The urban setting will not be to everyone's taste, although the nearby countryside is very beautiful. Dalyan is a much smaller, quieter resort surrounded by unspoilt rural scenery. As you would expect, the services and amenities on offer in Dalyan are more limited.

The recent designation of Dalaman as a so-called Tourist Development Area, has encouraged intense interest from developers. The state-sponsored plans include a golf course and several marinas,

relax...
you're with experts

TURKEY'S LEADING ESTATE AGENT
275 OFFICES NATIONWIDE
ESTABLISHED SINCE 1985

BODRUM TURYAP HEAD OFFICE :
Tel: 0 252 313 37 00-0 252 313 37 01
Email: bodrummerkez@turyap.com.tr

BODRUM GÜMBET TURYAP :
Tel: 0 252 313 55 65-0 252 316 45 65
Email: bodrumgumbet@turyap.com.tr

BODRUM BITEZ TURYAP :
Tel: 0 252 363 90 72 - 363 90 73 - 363 70 74
Email: bodrumbitez@turyap.com.tr

BODRUM GÜNDOGAN TURYAP :
Tel: 0 252 357 76 66 - 0 252 357 71 01
Email: bodrumgundogan@turyap.com.tr

TURGUTREIS MARINA TURYAP :
Tel: 0 252 382 43 17 - 18
Email: turgutreismarina@turyap.com.tr

BODRUM YALIKAVAK TURYAP :
Tel: 0 252 385 55 85 pbx
Email: bodrumyalikavak@turyap.com.tr

MUGLA TURYAP :
Tel: 0 252 212 19 86
Email: mugla@turyap.com.tr

DATÇA TURYAP :
Tel: 0 252 712 91 88
Email: datca@turyap.com.tr

FETHIYE TURYAP :
Tel: 0 252 614 88 88 - 0 252 614 75 75
Email: fethiye@turyap.com.tr

MARMARIS TURYAP :
Tel: 0 252 413 16 01 - 0 252 413 03 60
Email: marmaris@turyap.com.tr

MARMARIS SITELER TURYAP :
Tel: 0 252 413 80 95
Email: marmarissiteler@turyap.com.tr

MILAS TURYAP :
Tel: 0 252 512 88 14-0 252 513 37 00
Email: milas@turyap.com.tr

TURYAP

WWW.TURYAP.COM.TR

your first stop for property
on the Turkish coast

29

Despite rapid increases over the last 3 years, prices are below those in the more established Mediterranean property markets

making this an area to watch.

The small resort of Göcek has gained a reputation as Turkey's top yachting center. Strict controls on development and the comparative scarcity of flat land have kept prices relatively high.

The town of Fethiye and the nearby resorts of Çalış, Ovacik and Hisaronu are one of the most popular spots for buyers from the UK. There is a wide variety of property on offer, from town-centre apartments to more secluded villas.

Kalkan is smaller and more up-market, with good access to nearby attractions, such as the beach at Patara. High demand for villa properties from mainly British buyers has pushed up property prices and fuelled a major building boom. The pretty seaside town of Kaş has a good choice of property, although the lack of a decent beach and the distance to the nearest airport puts some buyers off.

Kemer is a rather utilitarian purpose built resort set in some of the coast's most beautiful scenery. Favoured by German and, more recently, Russian buyers, nearby Çamyuva is popular with British.

Antalya is a large city with lots of modern apartments and some atmospheric houses in the old town. The Mediterranean resorts of Side and Alanya have excellent beaches with interesting sights and activities, such as the Roman theatre of Aspendos and white-water rafting, nearby. Belek is the country's premier golfing area.

The stone and cave houses of Cappadocia are one of the most unusual property choices in Turkey. Often hundreds of years old, extensive renovation is usually required.

PROPERTY PRICES

Despite rapid increases over the last 3 years, prices are below those in the more established Mediterranean property markets, such as Spain and Italy. Expect to pay £35,000-£75,000 for a two-bedroom apartment depending on the area, build-quality and facilities. Villa prices vary from £45,000 for a very basic three-bedroom house on an old complex, to well over £200,000 in the more upmarket resorts, such as Kalkan. Of course, there are also far more luxurious and expensive properties in places like Bodrum and Istanbul. To get a better idea of local prices consult our area guides.

Prices everywhere have increased dramatically over the last 3 years with most areas experiencing rises of 15-20% per annum, far more in some cases. For example, land prices in Dalaman - an area benefitting from extensive government investment- have increased by over 150% in 2004, while property prices are up 100%. However, these dramatic increases have now slowed.

Generally, prices look set to continue rising in the face of growing demand. The introduction of a mortgage system, scheduled for 2006, could also encourage this trend. On a local level, however, rises in some resorts are expected to slow as the market reaches a more mature stage. The scale of development, much of it chaotic and poorly planned, may also begin putting buyers off in some areas.

The Property Market
What you get for your money...

£15K: 1-bed apartment in the centre of Altınkum, which needs renovation

£20K: Cave house in Cappadocian village of Göreme. In need of complete renovation.

£28K: 1200m2 plot of land near Belek with 20% building permission.

£32K: 2-bed apartment in a complex in Kuşadası. Completion date: spring 2006.

£35K: 2-bed off-plan apartment offered by developers in a complex with 2 pools in Altınkum

£40K: Old stone farmhouse in Üzümlü near Fethiye. Two-bed, 120m2. In need of extensive renovation.

£45K: 2-bed off-plan apartment near the beach in Alanya. 90m2 with communal pool and white goods included.

£55K: Small 2-bed apartment in the centre of Bodrum. 85m2 living area with views of castle.

£65K: 2-bed off-plan villa with pool in Çeş me.120m2 living area

£75K: Well-built 2-bed apartment with sea views near Side.125 m2 with shared pool.

£100K: 3-bed villa with garden in Çalış. 145 m2, 5 minutes walk to the beach.

£115K: Newly built, 3-bed duplex on a complex in resort of Içmeler, near Marmaris. 150m2 with communal pool.

£125K: Large 3-bed apartment with sea views in residential area near centre of Antalya.

A new apartment complex with shared pool in the resort of Hisarönü.

A newly-built four-bedroom villa in Ocavik, near Fethiye.

Houses on the Bosphorus in Istanbul typically sell for over £1 million.

Apartments on a complex with shared pool in Didim.

Prices vary hugely from £15K, to over £1 million on the Bodrum peninsular or in Istanbul

£160K: Off-plan 3-bed villa in Ovacik, Fethiye.130m2 with private garden & pool.

£170K: Luxury 4-bed villa on a development of 8 properties near Çeş me.

£200K: 4-bedroom villa with garden and sea view in the Karagözler area of Fethiye.

£215K: Renovated 3-bed stone house with private pool near Bodrum.

£235K: Luxury 3-bed villa with pool and jacuzzi overlooking Kalkan.

£250K: 4-bedroom villa with garden and pool near Göcek.

£300K: 3500m2 of land with 10% building permission near beach in Gümüşlük village, Bodrum peninsular.

£350K: Atmospheric 4-bedroom stone villa with pool, set in orchards near Yalıkavak, Bodrum Peninsular.

£525K: Luxury 6-bed seafront villa near Bodrum. Private pool, garage and large garden.

£750K: 5-bedroom villa with small garden in an upmarket residential district of Istanbul.

+£1 million: 4-bedroom waterside house overlooking the Bosphorus in Istanbul

GettingThere

Getting to Turkey in summer is easy with lots of charter flights to choose from. Out of season the options are more limited.

WHICH AIRPORT IS CLOSEST?

Turkey is a 3.5 hour flight from the UK.

(Resort/Area: Nearest airport)

Alanya: Antalya
Altınkum: Bodrum
Ayvalık: Izmir
Bodrum: Bodrum
Çeşme: Izmir
Datça: Dalazman
Fethiye: Dalaman
Göcek: Dalaman
Kaş: Dalaman
Kalkan: Dalaman
Kemer: Antalya
Kuşadası: Izmir
Marmaris: Dalaman
Side: Antalya
Cappadocia: Kayseri or Nevşehir

FERRY BOOKINGS:

Alternative Travel: Tel 08700 411448 www.alternativeturkey.com

Or visit: www.ferries.gr/mesline/ www.ferries.itgo.com

WHAT YOU NEED TO BRING YOUR CAR INTO THE COUNTRY:

✔ Valid Passport
✔ International driving license
✔ Registration documents
✔ International green card (Insurance)

See page 62 for information on visas, residency and work permits.

MOST PEOPLE travelling to Turkey do so by plane. During the summer season there are hundreds of package flights into the coastal airports of Bodrum, Dalaman and Antalya (see the Directory). However, most operators do not offer services in winter, when you must rely on scheduled flights.

Turkish Airlines and British Airways have daily flights, year-round to Istanbul. From Istanbul there are connecting flights operated by Turkish Airlines and other private airlines (see the Directory) to regional airports, such as Izmir, Bodrum, Dalaman and Antalya for the coastal resorts, or Kayseri and Nevşehir for Cappadocia. Cyprus Turkish Airlines operate a useful year-round service direct to Antalya, Dalaman and Izmir from Gatwick, Heathrow, Glasgow, Stansted.and Belfast, with the planes continuing to North Cyprus afterwards. Seats on scheduled flights can be booked through a specialist travel agent, such as *Alternative Travel & Holidays, Tel 08700 411 448, www.alternativeturkey.com*

There is much talk about new direct scheduled and charter flights in winter into Antalya and Dalaman, but as yet there isn't sufficient demand to support such services. This may change in the next few years as the number of British home owners increases and winter activities, such as golf, grow in popularity.

DRIVING TO TURKEY

It is about 3,000 km from London to Istanbul with the exact distance depending on the route you take. The northern option passes through Belgium, Germany, Austria, Hungary, Romania, Bulgaria, with a considerable distance still remaining to the south coast once you cross the Turkish border. Alternatively, you can pass through France and Italy, where there are car ferries from Ancona and Brindisi to the Turkish port of Çeşme. Ferries run throughout the year, although the service is very limited in winter. It is advisable to book in advance at any time.

ENTRY VISA

A 3-month tourist visa will be issued when you arrive in Turkey. It costs £10 for British citizens and is stuck into your passport.

try turkey

Villas, Apartments and Bungalows

New, re-sale and off-plan Villas and Apartments from £35,000.

We build and sell our own high specification apartments. We are an independent company who only deal with quality Developers. All our property is guaranteed for five years.

We operate a 'rent back' scheme on all purchases of our own properties. For full details on this scheme please contact us!

As an independent company we will research all properties to suit your budget and personal requirements then present you with a portfolio of suitable properties on your arrival in Turkey.

Try Turkey is a UK based company with offices and staff in both England and Turkey.

Contact us for rental properties in the Fethiye area.
Assisted 'Buying Trips' available.

We do not pass you onto any other company or agent but deal directly with you ourselves.

Buying Property

GettingStarted

Careful preparation before you start looking for a property can save you time and help you avoid problems later

At A Glance
Before You Start

✔ Decide on the property type you want.
✔ Set a realistic budget, not forgetting to include purchase costs.
✔ Decide on the areas you want to start looking by reading the area guides in this book.
✔ Research further into each area on the internet
✔ Make the necessary financial arrangements for the purchase.
✔ Make contact with a Turkish solicitor.
✔ Organise to view some properties with a local agent or developer.

BEFORE YOU BEGIN your property hunt in Turkey you should decide exactly what you are looking for. This sounds obvious, but clearly identifying your goals before you start looking can save a lot of time later.

Firstly, are you buying primarily for your own use or as an investment? Do you want a rental property or a holiday home? Are you looking for a peaceful rural retreat, or an apartment on a complex ? Will you be using the property out-of-season? Do you need to be close to an airport? Will you have a car, or can you rely on public transport? Do you want the company of other foreigners or would you prefer to immerse yourself in the local culture?

The answers to these questions will help you get off on the right track and find a property more easily. In order to focus your mind, it may be helpful to compile a list of exactly what you are looking for, and what you definitely do not want.

The area guides in this book are designed to give you information about the most popular places to buy property in Turkey. But there is no substitute for getting out there and exploring yourself. Before you leave you can do lots of research on the internet too. Try visiting some of the websites listed in the Directory.

Once you begin looking you should visit several areas at different times of the year, to get a real picture of what they are like. The coastal resorts are much more crowded in the summer and there is more traffic on the roads. On the other hand, public transport will be better in season, with more frequent buses and minibuses to the shops or beach. It may be harder to get around without your own transport in winter. Also, off-season many restaurants and shops close in the smaller resorts, leaving whole areas like ghost towns. There will be fewer foreigners around, if you want company. If you intend to use your property as a holiday home, these things may not trouble you. But if you plan to relocate permanently they should definitely be considered.

Many Turkish resorts have grown so rapidly that the basic infrastructure, such as access roads and storm drainage, have failed to keep pace. Some areas may be subject to flooding during the winter rains and dirt roads can become impassable due to mud. A brief visit in summer won't alert you to any of these potential problems.

If you are relocating permanently then consider renting an apartment so you can get to know an area really well before taking the plunge. You may also need to consider access to medical care or good schools if you have children. At the very least you should spend a couple of weeks in the place you intend to buy, getting to know it and comparing it to other areas.

Another excellent way to find out about an area is to talk to people who have already bought there. Most people will be only too happy offer advice. You can do this without even leaving home by joining one of the local forums that are springing up on the internet (see the Directory).

SETTING A BUDGET

Another important task before you begin looking for a property is to set yourself a budget. This should be realistic both in terms of your personal financial situation, but also with regard to actual prices currently being paid on the ground in Turkey. No use setting yourself the unrealistic goal of buying a luxury apartment with sea views for £20,000! Rather than wasting your time, consult the typical prices in the area guides section of this book, which will give you an idea of the current prices being paid in each area. However, you should remember that prices are rising extremely rapidly in many resorts, so these prices should only be used as an intial guide. Another good way to check prices is to visit the website of a local estate agent.

If you are buying a resale or old property it is important to include the costs of all necessary renovation work in your budget. The property should also be assessed by a builder or architect before embarking on the purchase, so you know what you are getting yourself into. Ask them to quote for the necessary work, but be wary of underestimating the time and expense of whatever is involved.

When setting your budget you should also factor in the costs involved in the purchase, such as legal fees. More details can be found on page 57.

If the property is unfurnished you will also have to include the cost of furniture in your budget. Furniture is much cheaper than in the UK, but kitting out a whole villa or apartment from scratch can still be costly.

ORGANISING THE FINANCING

Once you have set your budget, it is a good idea to organise the necessary financing, so the money for the purchase is ready should you decide to buy. Acting quickly is important due to strong demand in some areas and the rapid turn-over of properties. To avoid disappointment you should have a deposit ready, and have arrangements in place for funding the rest of the purchase. For more information about the cost of buying see page 57.

FINDING A SOLICITOR

It is advisable to have an independent Turkish solicitor look after your interests and make the necessary searches before embarking on any property transaction. Often buyers don't see the need for a solicitor, and many sales go smoothly without one. However, there are many potential pitfalls in the buying process. Having said that, merely appointing a Turkish solicitor is not enough. It is essential to find one who has experience of property law and who has dealt with purchases involving foreigners before. Speaking English is also important, so you can communicate easily with one another.

The British Embassy in Ankara has a list of English-speaking solicitors on its website: *www.britishembassy.org.tr*

The British Law Society also has details for accredited law firms in Turkey online at:
www.lawsociety.org.uk/choosingandusing/findasolicitor.law

RECENT CHANGES
TO THE PROPERTY LAW

In May 2005, the Turkish Constitutional Court annulled Article 19 of the recently introduced property law, which allowed, amongst other things, for foreigners to buy property in rural areas. The reason for the annulment was concern that some reciprocal agreements, allowing Turkish people to buy property in countries whose citizens can buy in Turkey, were not in place. There was also concern that large areas of farm land were being bought up by foreign individuals and companies.

The Turkish parliament is currently in the process of preparing new legislation, which will address these concerns. But the vast majority of foreign buyers have nothing to worry about, as most European countries, including Britain, have reciprocal agreements in place with Turkey. The expected changes will also not affect the right to buy within municipal areas. The new legislation may, however, limit the amount of land that can be bought by a foreign national in rural areas (currently 30 hectares), but any changes will not be retrospective, so there is no risk to property or land that has already been bought.

Newvs.Resale

New properties may be better built and have more facilities, but resale are often cheaper and may have the best location

At A Glance
New vs. Resale

RESALE PROPERTIES
Pros:
✔ May be in a better location
✔ Generally cheaper
✔ May have more character
Cons:
✘ Often need renovation
✘ May not meet new building regulations
✘ More difficult to sell

NEW PROPERTIES
Pros:
✔ Meets building regulations
✔ Ready for use
✔ More easily sold
Cons:
✘ Often more expensive
✘ May have less character

BUILDING STANDARDS have improved enormously in Turkey in recent years. These improvements are due to tighter building regulations and a new inspection regime, brought in by the government in the wake of the devastating 1999 earthquake. Rising expectations on the part of Turkish buyers are also encouraging improvements, while more buildings are now being built to meet the higher demands of the foreign market too. Due to these improvements there is often a big difference in quality between resale properties, say over 3 years old, and newer apartments or houses. The main reason people choose older properties is because they are often cheaper than new-builds. Built first, they may also have the best position, nearer the sea or with an uninterrupted view. However, even in the coastal resorts, most resale properties were built according to local tastes. For example, they often have more rooms in a given area and may feel cramped. Opening up the space by removing internal walls can solve this, though you should consult an architect or builder before buying.

Be aware that some older apartments and villas may not meet the new building regulations, particularly for earthquake resistance. The quality of finishing may also be inferior to new-builds, and older resale properties often need extensive renovation, which must be factored into your budget. Once again, a local builder should be brought in to give you a quote before proceeding with a purchase.

Although labour and materials are far cheaper than in Britain, the cost of renovating can add up to the difference in price between an old and a new property. Competition from new-builds may mean that you have difficulty selling an older property too.

Although labour and materials are far cheaper than in Britain, the cost of renovating can add up to the difference in price between an old and a new property

Apartments&Villas

A private villa with a swimming pool is the dream for many buyers, but apartments have a lot going for them too

MOST TURKISH PEOPLE live in apartments but developers are also now building more apartment complexes aimed specifically at foreign buyers in all the main resorts. These new developments are typically higher quality with more attention to fixtures and details.

Apartments are an increasingly popular choice with foreign buyers for a number of reasons. Firstly, they are normally cheaper than villas, making it easier to raise the necessary finance. They are also more convenient as general maintenance and communal gardens are normally looked after for you. Apartment complexes may also have security and shared facilities such a swimming pool and tennis courts. This makes them particularly popular holiday-lets, and they can provide excellent rental returns.

Communal services and maintenance are paid for by a monthly service charge, which is set at the beginning of the year. Known as an *aidat* in Turkish, this monthly charge may also include the cost of fuel oil or coal if the apartments have communal heating in the winter. There is often a caretaker, or *kapıcı*, living on-site who takes care of maintenance and the day-to-day running of the buildings.

The main drawback to apartments is that they offer less privacy and less space than a house, typically 80-125 m2. Private outdoor areas are often limited to a balcony or small terrace.

Prices vary between apartments in the same block. Units on the top floors may have better views and sell at a considerable premium. However, being on the top floor is very inconvenient if there isn't a lift. On the other hand, ground floor apartments may be darker and less secure, although direct access to a garden or communal area can add significantly to their value.

Villas are available for sale in all the coastal resorts. Naturally, they vary greatly in size, facilities and the quality of build. Some are little more than concrete boxes, while other building companies are producing high-quality properties with luxuries, such as marble flooring, air-conditioning and infinity pools.

Although they offer a greater degree of privacy, and generally have a garden, often with a swimming pool, villas can be expensive to maintain, particularly if they are empty for most of the year. Villas are also less secure than apartments, although property crime is quite rare in Turkey. You may also have to employ a management company, adding to your costs.

Buying a detached or semi-detached villa on a complex removes many of the drawbacks mentioned above. The property is looked after while you are not there, and you benefit from shared facilities like tennis courts and large swimming pools. In many areas, villas on complexes are easier to rent as families on holiday prefer to stay somewhere with these facilities.

At A Glance
Apartments
vs. Villas

APARTMENTS
Pros & Cons:
✔ Normally cheaper
✔ Easier to maintain
✔ May benefit from communal facilities
✔ Better security
✔ Higher rental potential in some areas
✔ Communal atmosphere
✘ Smaller living space
✘ Less privacy
✘ Limited private space outdoors

VILLAS
Pros & Cons:
✔ More living space & privacy
✔ Private outside space
✔ Good rental potential in some areas
✘ More expensive
✘ Higher maintenance costs
✘ Less secure

A Buyer's Tale
New-build Dreams

During a holiday in Ölüdeniz in August 2004, Peter and Liz Dasey decided to have a look at some of the new build villas around Fethiye.

"Our main motivation was to have a holiday home," says Peter. "Although we also wanted it to be a good investment." They particularly liked the atmosphere of Ovacik, and had been back with their three kids on holiday several times. They organised some viewings with a local developer who had a selection of villas and apartments on the slopes about the resort. Located in a quiet neighbourhood, but within walking distance of restaurants and entertainment, the couple were immediately impressed.

"We liked the properties on offer, which seemed really well-designed," says Liz. "Plus all the questions we asked the sales staff got straight-forward answers," adds Peter.

Peter and Liz also spoke to other people who had bought on the development and other nearby complexes built by the same builder. "They satisfied us that the construction company had a good track record," says Peter.

They made the decision to buy a three-bedroom, three-bathroom villa with its own swimming pool. Like all new-build properties in Turkey, the

Peter and Liz bought from Hanel Houses, www.hanelhouse.com

> "I would recommend signing-up with a local agency to handle the rental side"

villa came with a 5-year guarantee covering materials, fixtures and fittings. "This gave added piece of mind," says Peter.

The complex has 24-hour security and maintenance staff, who look after the properties and communal areas. There is a monthly service charge of £65 to pay for this. The couple plan to rent their villa through a local management company, keeping a four-week block each summer for themselves. Rather than making money out of the villa, their aim is for the rental to cover the running costs.

"I would recommend signing-up with a local agency to handle the rental side," advises Peter. "Unless you have the time to really promote the property yourself."

Buying Off Plan

Buying off-plan has advantages for the purchaser, but stick with a company that has a good track record of previous developments

An artist's impression of an off-plan villa development

BUYING OFF-PLAN IS INCREASINGLY POPULAR in Turkey, as elsewhere. As the name suggests, this method of purchasing involves making a commitment to buy a property that has yet to be built. Selling off-plan is popular with developers as it reduces the financial risks of a project. This advantage is passed on to the buyer as a discounted price, often significantly below the market value of the completed property. In a country like Turkey where property prices are rising rapidly, the buyer also benefits from the growth of his capital investment during the building period. Over a typical building period this can amount to 15-20% or more.

The buyer bases their decision to purchase off-plan on information provided by the developer or estate agents. This information should include a detailed description of the location; a site plan and details of communal facilities and a floor plan and building specifications. There should also be a schedule for when the various stages of the construction will be completed.

The buyer then secures the property by paying a deposit, typically 10-15% of the total price, at the time of entering into a contractual relationship with the developer. As with any type of legal contract, it is wise to have an independent Turkish solicitor examine the

Expert View
Buying Off-plan

Is buying off-plan popular in Turkey?
Buying off-plan has become extremely popular along the entire Turkish coast. In Alanya, I estimate that 60-70% of the properties now being sold are off-plan, with most of these bought primarily for investment purposes.

What are the advantages of buying off-plan?
Purchasing off-plan, at a price below the market value of the property, gives the buyer the chance for greater capital appreciation.

The earlier you buy into a project, the greater the potential returns.

Are there any drawbacks to purchasing off-plan?
Obviously apartments and villas

can't be built overnight and it may take up to 18 months for a property to reach completion. This isn't an issue for most investment buyers, but it can be a problem if you want a holiday home for immediate use.

What about the quality of construction in Turkey?
Huge steps have been taken by the Turkish government in the last three years to improve standards and regulate the building industry more tightly. On the ground this means regular inspections to check on the materials being used and

document before signing. They will also check that the developer either owns the land or has authority to develop on the land, and that all the necessary planning permissions are in place.

Generally speaking, off-plan contracts set out the builder's responsibilities and the schedule of payments. Payment is usually in instalments and may be due on dates specified in the contract. Alternatively, payments may be linked to the completion of particular stages of the building process. This gives the buyer security, allowing them to withhold payment if work has not been completed, or if the work is not to the standard specified in the contract. It is a very good idea to personally inspect the property before releasing the final payment, as getting a builder back once the last instalment is paid can be difficult. As an added incentive to get the job done on time, some developers are now including a penalty clause, with payments made to the purchaser if the building isn't completed on time. By law construction companies must give a 5-year guarantee on materials.

It is a good idea to opt for a developer who has already completed several similar developments, and, if possible, visit one of them for a look around. While you are there, you may even get the chance to talk to one of the owners. Although a good track record doesn't provide a guarantee, it does give an indication that the developer is reputable and it also gives you an idea of the standard of their work. You can also ask your solicitor to check whether the developer is

> Selling off-plan is popular with developers as it reduces the financial risks of a project. This advantage is passed on to the buyer as a discounted price.

the way thing are being done. We are confident that our properties, for example, would meet EU regulations.

What advice would you give people thinking of buying off-plan in Turkey?
If you are serious about buying off-plan, or any type of property for that matter, it is really important to do your homework. Research into the area you are thinking of buying, find out what it has to offer and the general prices. It is also good to have an idea of how the buying procedure works.

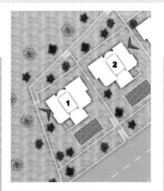

Building well is not an easy thing to do, so pick a company with a solid track record of previous developments. Ask for references, so you can talk directly to previous clients. Look at the payment structure

being offered and make sure that it is favourable for you. The constructor should offer a guarantee on materials and ideally the contract should also include a penalty clause, so you receive compensation if the building is not ready on time. Above all, you should feel confident that the company have answered all your questions and addressed any concerns. If for any reason you don't feel completely happy, then don't proceed.
Colin Twells is Director of Sales at M&C Property
www.mandcproperty.com

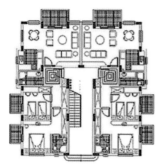

Properties on well-established cooperative developments can be excellent value for money

registered with the local chamber of commerce, although, once again, this is no guarantee.

It is also important for your solicitor to check on the title of the land on which the development is taking place. Ideally, the land should be owned by the developer, as this removes the chance of a disagreement between the builder and the land owner affecting the progress of the development. If the land is owned by a third party, your solicitor will have to be satisfied that there is a clear and legally-binding agreement between the two parties, or that the developer has a power of attorney to sell the properties on behalf of the land owner.

If the property you are buying off-plan is part of a complex, you should ask for a copy of the complex rules and enquire about service charges.

COOPERATIVES

Without a mortgage system the only way many Turkish people can afford a house, or holiday home, is to buy into a cooperative development. "Construction cooperatives", as they are officially known, are a recognised legal entity, which can buy land, build and act on behalf of its members. Similar to the off-plan concept, when someone joins a cooperative they make staged payments, often over a period of many years, towards the construction of the project. As a member they own a clearly defined part of the development, and a share of any communal facilities. However, actual title deeds to the individual properties are only issued when the entire development is finished and the members decide to dissolve the cooperative. Not being able to have a title deed for such a long time puts most foreign buyers off buying into cooperatives.

Many solicitors and estate agents also recommend against buying into cooperatives because of the potential for disputes between the various parties (the cooperative, the builder and the land owner) involved, and the possibility that construction costs on such large projects can escalate beyond initial estimates. These are not issues for concern if you buy a property on a completed cooperative development, where individual title deeds have been issued.

Properties on well-established cooperative developments can be excellent value for money. However, the poor quality of the buildings can mean that an extensive refit is necessary. Remember to get a quote for any necessary work before committing yourself. You may also find that cooperative properties are closer together and have less privacy than developments aimed at foreign buyers.

Cooperatives sometimes have excellent facilities, such as a swimming pool, cafés and shops, which are paid for by a monthly or annual service charge. Most of your neighbours will probably be Turkish families, which is perfect if you want to immerse yourself in the local culture. Remember to check the rules of the development, the service charges and any other responsibilities of the individual property owners before proceeding with a purchase.

Old Houses&Renovation

Renovation projects can be found in rural areas, as well as towns and cities like Ayvalık, Antalya and Istanbul

OLD HOUSES & RENOVATION

Old houses are fairly rare along the southern coast of Turkey. This is because historically the coastal region was sparsely populated and comparatively poor, and there simply weren't that many solidly built large houses. Traditional stone buildings are also expensive to construct and maintain, and impractical compared to the concrete homes that have replaced them. Unvalued by many Turkish people and without any official protection until comparatively recently, the old buildings that did exist were left to fall down or be demolished. In some areas earthquakes have also contributed to this process. There are some notable exceptions where historic buildings survive in greater numbers, such as the old neighbourhoods of Antalya and the Aegean town of Ayvalık (see pages 83 & 112), but generally old buildings are hard to find along much of the Turkish coast.

Istanbul, on the other hand, has far more old properties. The wooden houses, or *yalı*, along the Bosphorus are highly sought after and extremely expensive. More affordable are the old apartments in the inner-city areas of Beyoğlu or Galata. In Cappadocia, in central Turkey, the local people have traditionally lived in cave houses, and these have become popular renovation projects in recent years (see Cave Living, page 122).

Buying an old property can take far longer than a new one due to the complex ownership rights that are often encountered (see Labour of Love, Page 113). It is common for old properties to be owned by several members of the same family. In such cases, each person will need to be present at the registry office, or to have given power of attorney to a solicitor acting on their behalf, before the sale can proceed. This can cause enormous practical problems, particularly if the various family members live in different parts of the country or even abroad.

Before proceeding with the purchase of an old property it is wise to have a builder or structural engineer check the building and quote for any renovation work. Despite low labour and material costs, renovating an old property is expensive. In houses over a certain age, all the wiring and plumbing will almost certainly need to be replaced - or there may not even be any! Major structural work is also not unusual.

Your solicitor will need to find out if the house is in a conservation area, or *sit alanı*. In these areas of archaeological or environmental importance there are strict controls on any kind of building or renovation work. Your plans may have to be passed by the *Çevre Koruma Kurumu*, the government department in charge of managing officially protected areas, as well as the local planning committee. As with a newer resale property, your solicitor will also need to check that there are no outstanding debts against the title.

Despite low labour and material costs, renovating an old property is expensive

Land&Building

Buying a plot of land and having a property built on it is a popular option - although it won't happen overnight

BUILDING COSTS
Turkish construction companies can normally give you a cost per square meter for building in a particular area. Building costs vary depending on the type of terrain, the slope and the accessibility of the land where you intend to build. Of course, the type and quality of materials used in the building is also important, with extensive use of wood or imported materials likely to substantially increase the cost. As a rough guide, construction costs range from £350-£750 per m2, with a small swimming pool costing from £5,000.

SOME PEOPLE DECIDE TO BUY a plot of land and have a house or villa built on it. The availability of land suitable for building varies enormously from place to place. In some areas the supply of undeveloped land is nearly exhausted, with any available plots immediately snapped up by local developers. Elsewhere, for example where new areas have recently been opened up for development by municipalities, there is more choice. Needless to say, prices vary enormously depending on a multitude of factors, including location, access, availability and the density of building permitted on the land.

Building density relates to the base area of a building and does not include terraces, driveways or swimming pools. Maximum building densities vary from as little as 5% on agricultural land, to 25%, 30% or higher in urban areas. There may also be local restrictions on the height of buildings, particularly if it is close to the sea. If the land is in a conservation area additional restrictions may also apply.

Universal restrictions include a ban on owning land within 100 metres of the sea. Legislation introduced in 2003 allows foreign nationals up to 30 hectares of land in rural areas, although this law is currently being redrafted (see page 37) and it is widely expected that this limit will be reduced.

As part of their searches, a solicitor will look into any land-use, planning and building restrictions that apply to a piece of land. They will also make sure that the boundaries are clearly defined and that the plot you are buying is where it is supposed to be. This may sound strange, but it is not unheard of for people to discover that the land they bought is not exactly where they thought it was. If the boundaries are unclear your solicitor may recommend employing a surveyor.

Like when you buy a villa or apartment, when you purchase land you will receive a title deed, or *tapu*. This describes the ownership of the land, its position, its size and its boundaries as they are recorded in the official land registry. Some isolated rural areas have not been surveyed by the *Tapu ve Kadastro Genel Müdürlüğü*, the government agency in charge of surveying. In these areas ownership is registered at the local level in the form of a traditional village deed, and there will be no official title deed at the land registry. Village deeds are legally recognised, although many solicitors warn against buying a property without an official deed, not least because difficulties can arise when the area is surveyed.

Before buying land in Turkey it is important to consider what is around it. If you are planning to build on your land, it is likely that the person who owns a neighbouring plot is thinking the same. Consider carefully the effect of their building on your property. For example, will it overlook your house or block your wonderful sea view.

BUILDING

Before you can start building you need to obtain the necessary planning permission. This requires submitting detailed plans of your proposed project to the municipal or provincial planning department. For this you will need the help of a Turkish architect and a team of approved professionals. In some cases a geological report must also be commissioned.

When you receive planning consent your architect can draw-up a schedule of works. This includes details of every material to be used in the structure, from the concrete to the floor tiles and light-fittings. This document forms part of your contract with the builder.

Once this is completed you are ready to find a building company to quote for the work. Your architect may recommend a builder, but it is wise to get quotes from several others too. Seek recommendations locally and also ask for references from previous clients. A contract, drafted or checked by your Turkish solicitor, should be signed by both parties before any work starts. The contract should detail payment terms, with staggered payments linked to physical progress on the building. A typical payment schedule will include payments on signing the contract; on completion of the concrete structure; on completion of internal and external works; on completion of the garden and landscaping, with a final payment due when the keys are handed over. If possible, negotiate for a small sum to be withheld for a certain period after the building is finished, in case any problems surface that require the builder's attention. Any amendments to the original plans or additional expenses must be added to the contract and signed by both parties.

Like anywhere in the world, some builders in Turkey can be unreliable. Building costs are low, but standards of workmanship are generally below those expected in Western Europe. This means you should visit the site as often as possible to check on what is being done. If you can't visit regularly then try to find someone you trust to keep an eye on things. It is also a good idea to set a regular schedule for progress reports from your builder by email or telephone. These reports should be accompanied by digital photographs.

Some construction companies offer a complete service from purchasing the land to drawing up the plans; applying for the necessary planning permission; constructing the building and even sourcing the furniture. This type of package is very convenient, particularly if you don't have the time to make regular visits. However, make sure that a clear contract is in place before you start.

Depending on the project, construction can take up to a year. However, in the coastal resorts a ban on building during the tourist season effectively shortens the year by four months, meaning things can take a lot longer. A scarcity of skilled workman in some of the resorts can also slow things down.

Once the building is complete, you or your builder will need to get an *iskan raporu* from the local authorities. This demonstrates that all permits and taxes have been paid, and all regulations followed.

The traditional unit for measuring land in Turkey is the *dönüm*, which is equal to about 1,000m2, or 1/4 of an acre.

EstateAgents

A good estate agent will help you find and buy the right property but you should be wary of "cowboys"

At A Glance
Viewing Tips

✔ Organise in advance to see a variety of properties in different areas.

✔ Explain carefully to the estate agent want you do and don't want.

✔ Allow yourself plenty of time at each property.

✔ Keep a notebook with you to jot down your thoughts.

✔ Use a digital camera to take pictures of the main features of each place.

✔ Get a local map to mark the locations of the various properties you see.

✔ Go back and walk around each of the properties yourself to get a better feel for what the areas are like.

✔ Talk to other foreign property owners in the area if possible.

TURKISH ESTATE AGENTS

Whatever type of property you decide to buy, you will probably use the services of an estate agent. A good estate agent will have a wide choice of properties and can provide valuable insights into the local market. Contacted in advance, they can arrange for you to view a number of properties in a limited space of time. But the services offered by most Turkish estate agents go far beyond those you would expect in the UK. They typically provide help with travel arrangements and residence permits, legal advice and, once you have bought the property, help buying furniture and getting the utilities connected. Many also provide a management service, should you want to rent out your property. Although many people use the solicitor recommended by their estate agent, you may feel more comfortable with an independent Turkish lawyer looking after your interests.

The recent property boom in Turkey has seen an explosion in the number of estate agents. Completely unregulated until very recently, many of the "estate agents" selling property were driving taxis or selling carpets last month. Make sure that you approach a well-established company with offices and a track record in the local area. Don't make assumptions about a company based on their website alone. Ask for references from previous clients and check that the agent has taken and passed the newly introduced estate agent's exam.

Reputable estate agents have started organising themselves into local associations in one or two places, such as Kuşadası, but as yet there is no nationwide trade association.

Turkish estate agents charge a set commission of 3% from both the buyer and seller. However, it is not unheard of for unscrupulous agents to charge far more. To help avoid this, check the prices of similar properties with other local agents.

UK ESTATE AGENTS

There are a growing number of UK-based companies selling Turkish property. These companies may offer a wider choice of property than Turkish agents in various different parts of the country. They generally have large websites giving details of properties that are currently available. If you haven't decided exactly where you want to buy this can be useful, saving you the time of contacting individual local estate agents in each area. British-based companies may also have a better understanding of your requirements and concerns, while some buyers simply feel more comfortable dealing with a company in the UK. Indeed, if you are buying through an agent in the UK, you may have legal recourse in a British court should something go wrong.

The premium Altinkum property company has a number of off-plan projects due for completion in 2006. Each presents fantastic opportunities for both investment potential and pure pleasure.

My Turkish Home
The Premium Property Company

Buying - Selling - Renting - Letting - Interior Design - Property Management

DILEK VILLAS

Your perfect starter home in the sun —just 10 x 3-bedroom, 2-bathroom, 3-storey villas set in communal land-scaped gardens, swimming pool, 500 metres from the beach.

Prices start from £60,000

AKBAY VILLAS

Stunning 3-bedroom detached villas with amazing sea views. Beach front location, wooded surroundings, leisure facilities on site.

Prices start from £80,000

ESMA VILLAS

Choose a standard design, or configure your own individual house design to create your ideal holiday home.

Prices start from £85,000

COMING SOON

Luxury low-rise 2- and 3-bedroom apartments and penthouses in sought after Yesilkent location.

Prices start from £40,000

For further information contact: My Turkish Home.

UK: 01733 344304
Altinkum : 00 90 256 8132330

info@myturkishhome.com
www.myturkishhome.com

A good estate agent will be able to show you a range of suitable properties

On the other hand, UK-based estate agents, particularly those who don't specialize in Turkish property, may have a less complete local knowledge of the areas they are selling in. They may also have an incomplete knowledge of Turkish property law.

Finally you should check on the commission being charged by the UK agent for their services, as this can, in some cases, be higher than what you would pay a Turkish estate agent for the same property.

VIEWING TRIPS

Many estate agents and developers offer viewing trips to potential customers. These are usually 3-7 days in length with the company typically organising airport transfers, an orientation tour of the area and viewings for a series of properties. Dinner and entertainment may also be laid-on in the evenings.

> Many estate agents and developers offer viewing trips to potential customers

Viewing trips are a very cost effective way of looking at property, with the cost of your flight and accommodation subsidised by the company. If you decide subsequently to purchase a property, most estate agents will also deduct the cost of the trip from the price. They are ideal if you have only limited time, or if you have decided to buy in a particular area or even a specific development. However, remember that going on a viewing trip puts you under no obligation to buy. Don't allow yourself to be pressurised in any way.

DIRECT SALES

It is possible to buy a property directly from its owner without an estate agent. In fact, this is very common amongst Turks, and relies on word of mouth or the classified ads in the newspapers. When you are walking around also look out for signs saying "*Sahibinden Satılık*" (For sale by the owner) in windows or by the roadside, which will usually give a contact telephone number for the owner.

However, unless you speak Turkish or have a good Turkish friend, buying direct is very difficult as you will probably not be able to communicate with the owner. There is also a common tendency for the price to rise if the owner knows they are dealing with a foreigner!

security
in buying
real estate

Protect your real estate investment with a name you can trust.

Just like Turkey has a long, rich history, Stewart has over a hundred years of experience protecting real estate investors, purchasers and lenders. As the global leader in title protection, Stewart offers investors in the Turkish real estate sector superior service and a suite of products including:

- Title research
- Title guaranty
- Escrow services
- Securitization services
- Asset management

Call Stewart today.

Your land. Our business. Worldwide.

Stewart International
Gayrimenkul Bilgi Sistemleri ve Yatırım A.Ş.
Yapı Kredi Plaza, C Blok, Kat:3/A
34330 Levent - Istanbul
+90 (212) 284 7273
+90 (212) 284 7370 fax
email: turkey@stewart.com

stewart
›international

http://international.stewart.com

STC
LISTED
NYSE

S&P
SMALL CAP
600

The Buying Process

Buying a property in Turkey can be very simple, but it is a good idea to be familiar with the main points of the procedure

A title deed, or *tapu*.

Foreign nationals buying property in Turkey must be approved by the military authorities

MOST PEOPLE ARE SURPRISED at how straightforward and quick the buying procedure is in Turkey. Once everything has been agreed, a property transaction between two Turkish people can be completed in an afternoon. For a foreign buyer it takes significantly longer only because of the need for official permission from the military authorities. Below is an outline of the main parts of the buying process.

PROPERTY SEARCHES

Your solicitor will need to conduct a search at the registry office (*tapu dairesi*) to confirm that the property belongs to the seller, or that they have the authority to sell it for someone else. They will also check that there are no outstanding debts or charges, restrictive covenants or pre-emption rights against the property. For both new and re-sale properties it is important to ascertain that all the appropriate planning regulations were followed and building permission was granted. The solicitor will also check that the property is not in a military restricted area, where foreigners are forbidden from owning land or property. You can also ask them to check on the status of adjoining land, if you are concerned about future development.

In normal circumstances all the searches and checks should take no longer than 3-4 working days.

DEPOSIT & CONTRACT

After the initial searches have been completed, it is normal to pay a 10-15% deposit to show your commitment and to hold the property during the military investigation process (see below). Payment of the deposit should be recorded in a contract, written in Turkish and translated into English, which is signed by both the buyer and the seller.

The contract will also give the agreed price for the property and also may include details of how the payment is to be made. Provisions for what happens in the event that the purchase does not go through should also be included in the document, which should be drafted by a Turkish solicitor experienced in property law.

Contracts for off-plan purchases (see page 42) will also contain other details, such as the payment schedule, the date of completion, a schedule of works and any guarantees.

MILITARY PERMISSION

Foreign nationals buying property in Turkey must be approved by the military authorities. Before granting permission for the sale to proceed, the staff at the military headquarters will run background

Land Registry officials in places like Alanya are used to dealing with sales to foreigners

checks to make sure that you are a person of "good character". This involves checking whether you have a record of serious criminal or terrorist activity. Minor offences should not generally count against you.

As part of the military permission process, the authorities also check that the property you intend to buy is not located in a military restricted zone. These areas are dotted across the country and may include land adjacent or near military bases or strategically important parts of the coast. The whole procedure usually takes about 12-14 weeks, although some estate agents and developers seem to be able to get approval faster.

In normal circumstances all the searches and checks should take no longer than 3-4 working days

COMPLETION

Once you have received the go-ahead from the military authorities you can proceed with the actual transaction. This is usually conducted in the local land registry office (*tapu dairesi*), although you can also perform the transaction in a Notary Public, in which case the title deeds for the property will be officially changed in the land registry at a later time.

Performed in the presence of a land registry official, the transaction involves the current title deed holder, or their legal representative, giving consent for a new title deed (*tapu*) to be issued in the buyer's name. By this point the money for the transaction should have already changed hands (see below). An interpreter should be present to translate during the entire procedure, so you understand exactly what is going on.

If you are buying your property in a foreign currency, such as euros, contact a recognised foreign exchange broker

As the legal owner, your name and details will now be on the title deed, a copies of which are given to you and kept at the registry office. Additional copies of the title deed can be ordered from the registry office for a small charge.

TRANSFERING THE MONEY

There are several options for transferring money to Turkey, aside from a briefcase full of cash (not recommended!). The best way is to open a Turkish bank account well before the date of completion. That way, you can transfer the funds for the purchase from your account in the UK by Priority Payment electronic transfer. You will need to go into your local branch and fill out a form, giving the name and address of the bank where the account is held; the account number and branch code. This transfer method costs about £25 and takes 3-5 working days, though sometimes considerably longer.

Then you will need to make a transfer from your Turkish account so that the money reaches the seller's bank account on the day of completion. The transfer of title will not normally take place until the cleared funds are in the seller's account.

Another alternative is to have your bank issue a banker's draft, a form of cheque, which can be sent by courier or even taken in person to the beneficiary. Remember that banker's drafts take time to clear once they have been paid into the beneficiaries account, so give yourself plenty of time.

Expert View
Buyers and The Law

Why is it advisable to use a Turkish solicitor?

When buying property in any country it is very important to have a qualified professional looking after your interests. As the Turkish legal system and buying process are quite different to those in the UK, it is advisable to appoint a good Turkish solicitor, experienced in property law, to work on your behalf. To avoid a number of potential pitfalls, before getting into a contractual relationship and committing yourself, thorough legal checks should be made on the property. Due to the nature of the buying process for foreigners, and the lengthy military investigation, a tight contract is also a must.

What advice would you give prospective buyers?

I recommend getting a general understanding of the buying process before you start. Being clear about what happens when, will help you deal with specific issues as they arise. It is also a good idea to make contact with a solicitor early on, so they can give you general guidance and be ready to start working on your behalf immediately when you find something. Look around well, comparing prices, locations and build-quality. Don't be pressured into making a rushed decision. Some sellers will try to get a deal as quickly as possible and may put pressure on you. We often receive anxious telephone calls from people telling us that if they don't act quickly they will lose the property. The necessary legal checks can be performed by a good solicitor in a very short time, so there isn't any reason not to have them done before committing yourself.

If you are buying your property in a foreign currency, such as Euros, contact a recognised foreign exchange dealer, like *Currencies Direct, Tel 020 78130332, www.currenciesdirect.com*, who generally give a better exchange rate and charge less commission than the high-street banks.

Remember to transfer enough money to cover the costs involved in the purchase (see page 57).

Granting power of attorney to your solicitor or another trusted person allows them to act on your behalf

OBTAINING A TAX NUMBER

Once you have purchased a property you need to register with the local tax office who will issue you with a tax identification number. Your solicitor can perform this for you following the exchange of title.

GRANTING POWER OF ATTORNEY

Granting power of attorney to your solicitor or another trusted person allows them to act on your behalf. This can be particularly useful if you don't have the time to return to Turkey at the points of the buying process that your presence is required. Of course, it also saves you spending money on air travel and accommodation.

A power of attorney can be drafted by a Turkish solicitor and will need to be notarised in your presence at the Notary Public. The document can also be drafted by a British solicitor, although it will then need to be ratified by the Foreign and Commonwealth Office (see the Directory) before being sent to Turkey. This is a simple

Are there any specific considerations when buying off-plan?

We are seeing more and more off-plan purchases these days. As these transactions demand a much longer time frame, with a number of staged payments, it is very important to have a Turkish contract, clearly translated into English so you understand it fully, in place before you start. It is also very important for your solicitor to establish that the developer is the legal owner of the land or that they have the authority to build and sell the property.

Is there anything to be particularly wary or careful of?

Recently we have seen a number of investment schemes promising very high rates of return from property transactions in Turkey. I would advise prospective investors to consider the risks involved in any investment very carefully. In the current market it is certainly possible to achieve excellent capital growth, but be realistic about potential returns. Be wary of anything that looks too good to be true and consult an independent Turkish solicitor before making a commitment.

Gurkan Özkan is a founding partner of Acacia International, a British-Turkish law firm. www.acacia-int.com

A Buyer's Tale
From Dreams To Nightmare

John Norris traveled to Turkey in August 2003 to look for a piece of land on which to build his dream holiday home. After two weeks he found the perfect spot, in a stunning location overlooking the sea. The plot was bought through an estate agent and John commissioned a local architect to draw up the plans for his villa and get the planning permission. He then had the architect produce a detailed building specification and agreed a price for the work with a local builder. "I couldn't believe how smoothly it went," says John. "From buying the land to drafting the plans and finding a suitable builder took less than four months." He had a contract prepared by a solicitor and once this was signed, he transferred the agreed sum to the builder's account. This is where things began to go wrong.

"I would call the builder to get progress reports," explains John. "And it all sounded like it was going to plan." But when John flew out to visit the site six weeks later, things were far less advanced than he'd been led to believe. The builder apologised for the slow progress, saying that he was working on three other sites too. He assured John that the villa would be completed before May, when building had to stop for the start of the tourist season. John

Instead of a finished villa, John was left with a building site

"With hindsight I was incredibly naïve and I ignored all the danger signs"

returned home satisfied that all was still on track. "Then two weeks later I got an email from the builder saying he had to buy additional materials, and could I send extra money, " remembers John. "I was worried, but it wasn't a huge sum so I transferred it."

In the following weeks John tried to call the builder, leaving messages, which were never returned. He then received an email saying that the villa was nearing completion, but that some extra money was needed to hire more workers to get everything done by the May deadline. "I was so happy that it was nearly finished that I sent

the money off without thinking." But when he flew out to supervise the finishing touches three weeks later, rather than a finished villa, there was just a deserted building site. To make matters worse, the builder said he was too busy to meet. "By now, I knew that things were badly wrong, so I called my solicitors." says John.

With the builder refusing to finish the villa and in clear breach of contract, they were forced to take the matter to court. "With hindsight I was very naïve and I ignored the danger signs," says John. "I wish I'd visited more regularly or got my builder to send digital photos."

enough process but takes significantly more time than using a local solicitor. Turkish solicitors may also be more familiar with the various types of power of attorney that are required.

BUYING COSTS
The costs of buying a property in Turkey are lower than in the UK. The main costs include a transfer tax of 3%, based on the declared value of the property (see below). This is usually shared equally between the buyer and seller, although a different arrangement can be made and set down in the contract.

A registration fee, also based on the value of the property, is paid by the purchaser when the deeds are transferred at the registry office. If you use a Notary Public, the fees are standard and vary from £100-£250 depending on the service provided.

If the sale was organised through an estate agent their standard commission is 3% of the sale price from both the buyer and the seller. This commission rate may be open to negotiation in some circumstances. Value added tax, or KDV in Turkish, only applies to properties bought at auction. You must also pay for compulsory earthquake insurance, which is about £35. Finally, don't forget to take into account your legal fees.

DECLARED VALUE VS. MARKET VALUE
You may notice that the value of the property on the official title deed, or *tapu*, is far lower than the actual price you paid for the property. Although illegal, under-reporting the value of property is a universal practice, which reduces the stamp duty and annual property tax paid to the government. In fact, the declared value, particularly of an older re-sale property, may be less than 50% of the actual market value.

Although the government will inevitably crack down on this practice, it is widely agreed that this will not be for some time yet. In the meantime, your seller won't take very kindly to an attempt to declare the market value of the property and increase his tax bill.

SETTING UP A TURKISH LIMITED COMPANY
Foreign nationals can buy property using a Turkish limited company set-up for the purpose. One advantage of buying through a company is that you avoid the time consuming military investigation procedure. A Turkish solicitor can help you establish the company, with set-up costs of about £1,500. There are also administration costs, such as the fee for preparing the end of year accounts. This option makes particular sense if you are planning to let the property, as you can benefit from the lower Turkish corporate tax rate and be able to off-set set-up and running costs against any profit. However, technically you may be liable to pay tax on the value of any time you use the property, which is treated as a benefit in kind by the Inland Revenue. Consult a tax adviser for information.

TYPICAL COSTS INVOLVED IN BUYING A £100,000 PROPERTY
Stamp duty (1.5%): £300
Land registry fees: £160
Notary Public fees (if used): £190
Earthquake Insurance: £36
Estate agent (3%): £3,000
Solicitor: £1,500-£2,500

The declared value, particularly of an older re-sale property, may be less than 50% of the actual market value

AvoidingTheCurrencyBlues

Phillip McHugh, Senior Executive Dealer at Currencies Direct, explains how one of the major causes of stress for overseas home buyers is overlooking the importance of the foreign exchange rate.

ALTHOUGH A DREAM FOR MANY, buying a property overseas can turn into a nightmare if vital parts of the buying process are neglected.

You would never dream of buying a house in the UK without knowing how much you were going to finally pay. So why, when buying abroad, is this exactly what many property buyers do? Whether buying a Turkish property outright or in instalments, the purchase may involve changing your hard earned cash into a foreign currency, probably euros. Unfortunately, no one can predict the exchange rate as many economic and political factors constantly affect the strength of the pound. Exchange rates are constantly moving and there is no guarantee that they will be in your favour when you need your money, so it is vital that you protect yourself against these movements. A lack of proper forward planning could cost you thousands of pounds.

The affect the exchange rate can have on the cost of your property can be seen if you look at what happened to the euro in the first ten months of 2004.

Sterling against the euro was as high as 1.5279 and as low as 1.4096. This means that if you were buying a property worth €200,000 it could have cost you as little as £130,898 or as much as £141,884, a difference of £11,000.

It is possible to avoid this pitfall by buying and fixing a rate for your currency ahead of time through a forward transaction. This is the Buy Now, Pay Later option and is ideal if you still have some time to wait before your money is due overseas or if you are waiting for the proceeds from the sale of your UK property. Usually a small deposit will secure you a rate for anywhere up to 2 years in advance. By doing this, you will have the currency you need at a guaranteed price and know exactly how much your dream home is costing.

If, however, you need to act swiftly and your capital is readily available then it is most likely that you will use a spot transaction. This is the Buy Now, Pay Now option where you get the most competitive rate on the day. Another option

High Street Bank vs Currencies Direct
How do they compare for regular currency transactions?

HIGH STREET BANK
€1,000 @ rate:1.4350 = £696.86
Commission 2% = £13.94
Telegraphic transfer fee £25.00
Total cost per month £735.80

CURRENCIES DIRECT
€1,000 @ rate:1.4750 = £677.97
Commission Free
Telegraphic transfer fee = £5.00
Total cost per month= £682.97
Saves you £52.83

*Figures are for illustration purposes only and may not reflect present rates or bank charges.

Currencies Direct helps you get more of your money

A Buyer's Tale

"Using Currencies Direct, we could have saved nearly £2,000"

Richard and Glauce Noble bought a four-bedroom villa in Kusadasi's Ladies Beach area in 2004. The sale price was agreed at €100,000, which they needed to send out to their solicitor. Once back in the UK, they organised the transfer into the solicitor's account through their local bank. At the rate of exchange given by the bank, the couple paid £69,686, plus a £25 wiring charge for their new villa. However, if they had gone through a foreign currency broker, such as Currencies Direct, they would have been given a better rate of exchange and paid only a £5 wiring charge, saving them nearly £2,000.

The Noble's could have saved almost £2,000 by using a foreign exchange broker

available if you have time on your side is a limit order. This is used when you want to achieve a rate that is currently not available. You set the rate that you want and the market is then monitored. As soon as the rate is achieved, the currency is purchased for you.

However, many of us do not have the time or the expert knowledge to be able to confidently gauge when the foreign currency rates are at their most favourable. This is where a foreign exchange specialist can help. As an alternative to your bank, foreign exchange specialists can offer you extremely competitive exchange rates, no commission charges and lower transfer fees. This can mean considerable savings on your transfers.

Even when you have bought your property you must not forget about foreign exchange. It is likely that you will need to make regular transfers from the UK, whether for mortgage payments, maintenance expenditure or transferring pensions or salaries, and using a foreign exchange specialist

can make sure that you get more of your money each time, even on small sums (see example, page 58). The high-street banks typically offer their customers a tourist rate of exchange due to the small amounts that you are transferring. Furthermore, banks will generally charge a wiring fee of £10-£40 for every transfer that you make. Many will also levy a commission charge of about 2%, which amounts to an extra £10 on a £500 transfer.

Foreign exchange specialists, on the other hand, are able to give a commercial rate of exchange regardless of the amount that you transfer. They also charge a lower fee (typically £5-£15) and no commission regardless of the size of the payment. The bottom-line saving when using a currency broker instead of a bank can be sizeable, as illustrated by the example opposite.

**To find out more contact
Currencies Direct, Tel 020 7813 0332,
www.currenciesdirect.com**

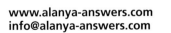

Living in Turkey

Visas&Working

For short stays all you need is a tourist visa, though if you plan to stay longer it's easy enough to get a residence permit

RESIDENCE PERMITS
What you need to apply for a residence permit
4 x Application forms
4 x Recent passport photographs
Passport
(with minimum one year validity)
Residence confirmation from your
Muhtar (elected local official)
Proof of income or savings
Your rental agreement or title deed
Application fee (see below)

RESIDENCE PERMIT FEES
1 year £415
2 years £1,200
5 years £2,140
Plus a £65 admin fee

IF YOU ARE ONLY VISITING TURKEY for short periods then you only need a tourist visa, which is issued when you arrive. A tourist visa is valid for three months during which time you can come and go as often as you like. The cost of a tourist visa for British citizens is currently £10, which must be paid in cash before going through passport control. Visa requirements for other nationalities can be found at:

www.mfa.gov.tr/MFA/ConsularInformation/ForForeigners

Many people who want to stay longer than three months simply leave and re-enter the country on a new tourist visa. This is simple in many of the coastal resorts where it involves little more than a day trip to one of the Greek islands. Staying in the country after your visa has expired will mean paying a hefty fine, calculated on the number of days you have overstayed, when you depart.

If you plan to stay in the country for extended periods you can apply for a residence permit. This involves a visit to the Foreigner's Section of the local police headquarters (*Emniyet Müdürlüği, Yabancılar Şubesi*). In the main tourist areas the staff will be used to dealing with European applicants, but don't count on anyone speaking English. It is a good idea to have a Turkish friend accompany you, or better still, your estate agent, a solicitor or a specialist local agency can deal with the application for you.

Your application is forwarded to the Ministry of Internal Affairs (*İçişleri Bakanlığı*) for processing, which usually takes about two months. The initial residence permit is valid for one year, after which you can apply for a two-year, then a three or five-year extension. The fees are £415, £1,200 and £2,140 for the one, three and five-year permits respectively, plus you need to pay a £65 administration fee. A document certifying that you live where you say you do will also need to be obtained from the *muhtar*, an elected official in charge of your village or neighbourhood. This is a good opportunity to introduce yourself as well. Finally, you will need to prove that you have a regular income

If you only plan to stay for short periods a tourist visa is all you will need.

A Buyer's Tale
No way back

Les and Sylvia Storey began thinking about living abroad after Les was made redundant in September 2002. A chance conversation with a colleague in Sylvia's office turned their thoughts to Fethiye as a suitable destination for a retirement home. She recommended talking to a local estate agent she had recently bought a property from. She also assured the Storeys that they could live comfortably on Les' pension. A telephone conversation with the estate agent and some research on the internet convinced them that Turkey was the right place for them. But with no spare funds to finance the project, the couple boldly decided to put their Northampton bungalow on the market, and within a few weeks it had been sold. The mortgage and other debts were settled and they moved into a rented cottage.

"We were quite worried at this point," remembers Sylvia. "That the remaining funds might not be sufficient to buy a property and leave us enough for 'a rainy day'."

But within two days of arriving in Fethiye the estate agents had managed to find a property within their budget. A four-bedroom detached villa with a small garden, it was located on a twelve property complex in the beach resort of Çaliş. Having

Les, Sylvia and Holly bought from Lagoon Estates www.lagoonestates.com

"I'm working harder than I ever did before," laughs Sylvia. "But I love it and it has given me a new lease of life."

started the buying procedure, the couple returned to Northampton to make final preparations for their move out to Turkey with their little dog Holly. Everything went smoothly with the move and despite the sadness of leaving their four grown-up daughters and friends, they quickly settled into life in their adopted country.

"The neighbours were very welcoming, " says Les. "And we enjoyed the relaxed lifestyle and weather after England."

The couple began exploring the area around Fethiye and Les kept himself busy in their new garden. Sylvia was also offered a job by their estate agent, who had become a friend.

"I turned it down because our intention was to retire and enjoy a relaxed life in the sun," says Sylvia.

But Sylvia soon found herself spending a few hours a week helping set up the company's new office. This gradually became full time and she is now a well-established member of the team.

"I'm working harder than I ever did before," laughs Sylvia.

"But I love it and it has given me a new lease of life."

By law, you must carry photo-ID, such as a passport, with you at all times in Turkey

or sufficient funds to support yourself in Turkey. This can be done with bank statements or a work contract. Your passport must be valid for the entire permit period also.

You can apply for a temporary residence permit at the Turkish Consulate in London before you travel. However, once you arrive you must still go through the same process to obtain a full permit, so there is little point in the extra work and expense involved.

A residence permit entitles you to live in the country but not work. If you intend to work or set-up your own business you will need to get a separate permit (see below). If you are shipping your household possessions, you will be liable for import duty unless you have a residence permit.

WORKING IN TURKEY

Many foreigners are employed by Turkish companies or choose to set-up their own businesses. In the coastal areas most employment is in the tourist industry, although with the current property boom there are also lots of jobs in real estate too.

Istanbul has far more diverse employment opportunities and wage rates are higher. However, the cost of living is also significantly higher than other parts of the country. Other large cities, like Izmir and Ankara, may also have a variety of jobs suitable for foreigners.

There is a long official list of occupations that a non-Turkish person cannot engage in, including tourist guide and photographer. Work in other fields, such as medicine, requires special permission.

Native English speakers are always in demand by private language schools and some Turkish universities. A degree and teaching qualification, such as a TEFL certificate, is generally required, although some schools may employ you without. Rates of pay are low by European standards, typically £400-£1,000 per month, depending on where you are and how much you work. But the schools often provide free accommodation and flights home on the successful completion of your contract.

To work in Turkey you or your employer will have to apply for a work permit (*çalısma izni*). The application process can take several months, or even longer, but you can normally start working while the application is in process. You can also apply in the UK at least 2 months before your departure. Further information can be found at: *www.turkishconsulate.org.uk*.

Foreign nationals can set-up a limited company in Turkey, with or without a Turkish partner. Talk to a Turkish solicitor, or find basic information on establishing a company at www.hazine.gov.tr/realsectorleg.htm

GettingAroundTurkey
Travelling from place to place without a car is easy thanks to an excellent bus network and domestic flights

DOMESTIC FLIGHTS

Turkey is a large country and flying is the fastest and most convenient way of travelling long distances. Turkish Airlines operate an extensive domestic network with flights from Istanbul and Ankara to all cities and most provincial centres. Services to the main cities, such as Izmir, depart regularly throughout the day. Smaller airports like Dalaman and Bodrum are served by fewer daily flights, which can become very booked up during the summer months and at peak times, such as at the weekend. Turkish Airlines allow unconfirmed bookings for domestic flights to be held open until 24-hours before departure, meaning that even if a flight appears full you have a good chance of getting a seat if you are put on the waiting list.

A number of private airlines now operate domestic routes from Istanbul but the services are less frequent than Turkish Airlines. These include Flyair, with flights to Antalya, Bodrum and Izmir, Onur Air, with destinations including Kayseri (Cappadocia), Antalya, Bodrum and Izmir, and Atlas who fly into Dalaman, Antalya, Bodrum and Izmir. Tickets range from £20-£45 one-way and can be bought online (see right).

DRIVING IN TURKEY

Thanks to huge investment the country's road network, particularly around the main cities and tourist areas, has improved greatly in recent years. The intercity highways are now mostly dual carriageway and the main coastal road has been widened for much of its length, cutting journey times and making driving far safer. Even so, driving in Turkey can be quite a challenge thanks to bad road conditions and the poor standard of many drivers. Reckless and dangerous manoeuvres, such as overtaking on blind bends, are not uncommon, as is reckless speeding. As most of the country's freight is transported by road, slow-moving, heavily laden trucks are another common hazard. Needless to say, the country's accident rate in very high, making careful, defensive driving a must. However, once away from the main towns and cities, the traffic is light compared to the UK and driving can be extremely pleasurable.

Breakdown cover and information about importing and driving your car in Turkey is available from the *Turkish Touring and Automobile Association, Tel 0212 2828140, www.turing.org.tr*

If you enter the country on a tourist visa, you can bring a car with you and drive it for a maximum of six months in any calendar year. Details of the car will be entered in your passport, and if you want to leave the country without the car during that time, it must be left at a customs office. You will be charged a daily parking fee for the privilege. In addition to your driving license you will also need the

AIRLINES
Turkish Airlines:
www.thy.com.tr
Online booking available
Alternative Travel:
Tel: 08700 411448 (UK)
www.alternativeturkey.com
UK ticketing agent
Atlas Jet:
Tel 0216 4440387
www.atlasjet.com/eng
No online booking
Flyair:
Tel 0212 4444359
www.flyair.com.tr
Online booking available
Onur Air:
Tel 0212 6629797
www.onurair.com.tr
Online booking available

ROAD SPEED LIMITS
120 km: Dual carriageways
90 km: Rural highways
50 km: Built-up areas

DOLMUŞ

Communal minibuses are the work horse of the Turkish transport system, ferrying people around in towns and cities, and in the countryside too. They operate fixed routes like a bus, but stop wherever passengers request – much to the annoyance of following motorists! The destination is usually posted prominently on the front of the vehicle and you pay the driver or his mate when you get on. Dolmuş in many of the resort areas like Bodrum operate 24-hours a day during the busiest summer months.

HOW LONG IT TAKES...BY BUS

(typical journey times)

Istanbul - Izmir: 8 hours
Izmir - Antalya: 7 hours
Ankara - Antalya: 8-9 hours
Izmir - Bodrum: 3.5 hours
Marmaris - Fethiye: 3 hours

Istanbul is well served by short-hop ferries across the Bosphorus and high-speed catamarans acroos the Sea of Marmara to Yalova and Bandirma. For timetables and prices visit: www.ido.com.tr

car's registration documents and an international green card from your insurance company.

Longer-term residents with a residence permit will need to re-register their car in Turkey and be issued with a blue number plate. To do this you will need a letter from your employer, a letter of guarantee from a bank, a valid residence and work permit. For full details visit the *Turkish Touring And Automobile Association website: www.turing.org.tr*. There are agents who can perform the necessary paperwork and application for you, and their small commission is well worth the money.

There is nothing to stop foreigners buying a car in Turkey, although prices for new and second hand vehicles are oftenhigher than in the UK. It is more economical to opt for a car that is manufactured in Turkey, such as Renault, as the parts are cheaper and more widely available. Petrol is very expensive in Turkey (see page 67), so running a car is a significant cost.

BUSES

Turkey has a very efficient private bus network with modern buses plying routes between towns and cities across the country. Because many people can't afford a car, buses provide the main form of long distance transport and are very reasonably priced. They are generally air-conditioned and passengers are served hot and cold drinks on-board. Smoking is not permitted anymore, although buses make regular stops for refreshments. Longer journeys are often taken overnight, although travelling by train or plane is more comfortable. On some routes you may have a choice of companies, including one of the premium carriers, such as Varan or Ulusoy. Journey times are significantly longer by bus than car (see left)

TRAINS

Turkish trains, except for the modern expresses operating between Istanbul and Ankara, are slow, old-fashioned and frequently late. But they are the most comfortable and fun way of travelling long-distance in Turkey. Run by the state-owned TCDD, the train network also only gives scant coverage of the country, with no line along the western Mediterranean or Aegean coasts. The only routes that may useful to property buyers are those from Istanbul's Haydarpaşa station to Ankara, and then Kayseri for Cappadocia. There is also a good over-night express between Ankara and Izmir.

FERRIES

Turkish Maritime Lines operate ferries along the Black Sea coast from Istanbul to Rize and back each week in summer. Potentially more useful for property hunters is the overnight service between Istanbul and Izmir each weekend. This departs Istanbul Friday evening, returning again from Izmir overnight on Sunday. Contact a Turkish Maritime Lines agent in Turkey to make a booking.

CostofLiving&Money

Lower prices for most things, except petrol, mean that your money goes alot further in Turkey

THE COST OF LIVING IN TURKEY is significantly lower than in Britain, and other Mediterranean countries, such as Spain and Greece. Prices for food and other consumable goods are much cheaper, while fresh produce is often grown locally and costs a fraction of what it does in the UK. However, there are marked differences in the cost of living across the country. Istanbul is the most expensive part of the country, but the cost of living is also higher in the coastal resorts. In these areas you can still dine out for £10-£15 per head in a good restaurant, or eat for a fraction of that amount in a local Turkish eatery. A typical weekly shopping bill for two is £40-£60, though it could be significantly more if you buy expensive imported goods.

Wage rates are very low in Turkey compared with Britain. A manual worker can expect to earn about £150 per month, while a school teacher takes home about £300 each month.

One of the things that is expensive in Turkey is petrol. For example, one litre of unleaded petrol is £1.05p, compared with 86p in the UK. Owning a car is a major expense, and one that may not be necessary if you are only using your property for holidays as public transport is so good.

TYPICAL TURKISH PRICES

A loaf of bread 25p
1 kg of tomatoes 20p
330ml can of beer 40p
1 litre of unleaded petrol £1.05

**OPENING A
BANK ACCOUNT**

To open a bank account you will need to visit a branch with proof of your Turkish address, such as a utility bill, and another form of photo-ID.

BANKS

The Turkish banking system has been reformed in recent years by privatisation and tighter regulation. Still, at the customer level red tape and petty bureaucracy can be much worse than in the UK. You will have a choice of banks in most towns, with big names such as İş Bankası, Ak Bank and Yapı Kredi on most high streets.

Before choosing a bank, it is a good idea to ask for recommendations from other foreigners locally. It is also wise to find out how much the banks charge for services such as receiving money transfers, as fees for these kind of things differ widely.

Although international banks such as HSBC have branches in Turkey, there is no advantage to choosing them over a Turkish bank. Even if you have an account with the same bank in the UK, international transfers are treated in the same way.

Banks in the main resorts will often have at least one English-speaking member of staff, although you may need the help of an interpreter or a bilingual friend for more complex affairs. Also remember that smaller branches may not be able to offer a full range of banking services, which could be necessary if you are planning to start a business.

Many ATMs can display in Turkish, English and other European languages

Cash dispensers are everywhere in towns and cities.

Old For New Money

The New Turkish Lira

On January 1, 2005 a new currency, known as the New Turkish Lira, or *Yeni Türk Lira* in Turkish, was introduced. Abbreviated as YTL, the new money replaces the old Turkish Lira, whose value had been eroded by decades of inflation to a point where even the price of a loaf of bread was hundreds of thousands. Thankfully, the new currency has six fewer zeros! The old currency is being withdrawn from circulation throughout 2005, but new and old money may be used until the end of the year. But don't panic after that, as you will be able to exchange the old notes at branches of the Turkish Central Bank (TC Merkez Bankasi) or TC Ziraat Bankasi. Old habits die hard, so you will probably here prices quoted in millions and billions for some time yet.

Turkish banks offer a range of current, savings and deposit accounts, with credit card, debit card and overdraft facilities usually available. Despite interest rates having dropped dramatically in recent years, the time-deposit accounts and investment funds offered by many banks can produce excellent returns. However, you won't be able to withdraw your money for a fixed term. You may prefer to open a foreign currency account, thereby protecting your money against any devaluation of the YTL. Most banks offer U.S. dollar, euro and sterling accounts, with some banks such as Garanti Bank (*www.garantibank.com*) offering dual currency accounts where your balance is held in foreign currency, but you can make payments and withdrawals in YTL. Most banks now offer internet accounts, so you can check your account balance; transfer money between accounts; make one-off payments or schedule regular standing orders online. Standard bank charges are levied on an annual or six-monthly basis, with extra charges for some additional services.

CASH MACHINES (ATMS)

Cash machines can be found all over Turkey with a wide choice of ATMs in most towns and resorts. Most ATMs can display in Turkish, English and other European languages. All operate with foreign credit cards and most with Maestro cards too. Most credit card companies and banks levy a charge for withdrawing cash. These charges can be as much as 2% of the amount withdrawn with a minimum charge of up to £2, so it is wise to withdraw a reasonable amount each time.

In addition to withdrawing money Turkish ATMs allow you to make deposits, pay bills and transfer money.

CREDIT CARDS

Credit cards are widely accepted in all but the smallest shops in Turkey. Many credit card companies make a small charge for each overseas transaction made. Once you have opened a bank account you may be offered a Turkish credit card.

BILL PAYMENTS

Regular payments for utility bills, maintenance charges or insurance premiums can be paid automatically from your Turkish bank account by completing a standing order form. It is a good idea to take your bill into the bank with you so that all the details are filled out correctly.

Most banks now also offer telephone and internet banking services including bill payment facilities. Despite this, some holiday home owners prefer to entrust bill paying to a local property management company or a friend.

REAL ESTATE TAX

Collected by local authorities, this annual tax is based on the declared value of your property or land, which may be substantially less than what you actually paid for the property. The rates are currently 0.2%-0.3% for land and 0.1% for residential buildings, with the payment collected in two instalments in March-May and November each year.

INCOME TAX

You have to pay tax on any income that you make in Turkey, from employment, investments or renting out your property. Income tax rates are banded according to your income and vary from 15%-40%.

Despite a pervasive culture of tax evasion, the Turkish authorities are slowly tightening up regulations in an attempt to raise more tax revenue. In the past, very few foreign property owners paid tax on their rental incomes, but a recent outcry in the press may well lead to a crack down on this practice. As a UK resident any income made on a property in Turkey would also be taxable by the British authorities. However, due to a double taxation agreement between Turkey and the UK, any income taxed in one country will not be taxable in the other. One advantage of buying a property with a Turkish company is the ability to offset any rental income against a large range of expenses related to the property.

CAPITAL GAINS TAX

As an individual you will be taxed on any increase in the capital value of a property only if you have owned it for less than five years. Companies paying corporation tax do not have to pay capital gains tax if they have owned the property for more than two years.

CORPORATION TAX

If you established a Turkish company to buy your property you will be liable to pay a corporation tax of 30% on any profits, including from rental income. In reality, you can offset the profit against any expenses you incurred, such as furniture, utility bills and maintenance charges. You will also have to pay capital gains tax if you sell the property within two years of buying it.

PENSIONS & BENEFITS

Moving abroad will not affect you state pension payments, however you will need to organise for the money to be transferred into your Turkish account. Bank charges on relatively small, regular transfers can become expensive, so think about pooling the money and transferring larger amounts less often. A British pension can support a comfortable lifestyle in Turkey due to the lower cost of living.

If you have not yet reached retirement age you may want to consider continuing to make National Insurance contributions after you move to Turkey. This will ensure you are entitled to receive a full UK state pension when you are eligible. Some other state benefits are payable to British citizens who move abroad, but you should check this with the Department of Works and Pensions before you make any plans.

PROPERTY INSURANCE

It is important to insure your Turkish property and all its contents. A typical household policy taken out with a Turkish insurer should include cover against damage or destruction of the building and its contents by fire and earthquake; cover against theft and accidental damage to furniture and third-party liability. The policy may also cover personal injury while at home. Some of the largest firms, like Axa Oyak, can provide the policy and other documents in English. A typical annual premium for a 100m2 apartment is about £60, but you should make sure that you have adequate cover for all possible eventualities. Finally, remember to check on the procedure for making a claim should it be necessary. For example, you may be required to notify the police and your insurance company within a certain time of a burglary. Proof of purchase may be required by your insurer for the replacement of stolen or damaged items or you may need to take digital photographs of high-value items.

Banks in the main resorts will often have at least one English-speaking member of staff

Services&Utilities

Getting water and electricity connected is a simple process, while gas and drinking water can usually be delivered to your door

Getting Connected

If you are buying a new or resale property it will usually already be connected to the mains water and electricity supplies. However, if you are having a house built or renovating an old property you may need to apply for a new connection. This could be costly if you are some distance from the nearest water main or electricity supply, so get a quote so you can factor the cost into your budget.

To get your utilities connected it is essential to have an *iskan raporu*. This is obtained from the local authority and is only granted when it is shown that all taxes and permit fees have been paid and that the building meets planning and building regulations. The developer or construction company will usually apply for this, but it may be worth checking. When you take over a property any outstanding bills need to be settled before you can change the electricity and water accounts into your name. To transfer the account you will need the title deeds or rental agreement, your passport and bank details.

TAP WATER IN TURKEY is chlorinated so it can be used for brushing your teeth, however, it is not recommended to drink. Instead you can buy bottled mineral water at shops and supermarkets. But it is far more economical, and environmentally friendly, to buy water from the local watershop. These supply spring water by the litre in large plastic containers. In towns and cities they will generally deliver to your door if you give them a call. Turks take water very seriously and people often travel long distances to fill up containers at a particular spring, whose water is judged to be particularly tasty or fresh. Mains water supplies are metered and water bills issued by the local water authority on a monthly or quarterly basis. Bills can be paid in person at the water company offices or at some banks. It is much more convenient though, to set-up a regular direct debit from your bank account. There is a penalty for not paying on time, and your supply will eventually be cut off. Huge increases in demand in some areas have stretched local water supplies to the limit. Periodic water cuts are common during the summer months. It is handy to keep a container of water in the bathroom for flushing toilets or washing hands. Be aware that there have been cases of water supplies to foreign-owned homes being siphoned-off by people in the vicinity. Although this is technically stealing, it seems to be viewed by some locals as a harmless "tax". To avoid this, keep an eye on your water bills and report any large increases in use to your water company.

ELECTRICITY

Most electricity in Turkey is supplied by the state-run company TEDAŞ. The supply is 220 volts and two-pin plugs, similar to those in other European countries, are used. With a suitable adapter, electrical appliances from the UK can be safely connected to the mains. As with water, demand for electricity is growing so fast that the network cannot cope in some areas. This means frequent black outs and fluctuating supplies. Apart from some candles, it may be wise to invest in a voltage regulator to protect computers and other sensitive equipment from power spikes. You may also consider investing in an uninterruptible power unit, which continues supplying electricity to sensitive equipment if there is a power cut.

NATURAL GAS

Apart from Istanbul, Ankara and some other cities with mains gas, natural gas for cooking and heating water is supplied in metal canisters. These are ordered from a local gas supplier, who will deliver it to your door. A full canister costs around £10 and lasts for 6-8 weeks when used for cooking. Empty canisters are exchanged for full ones when you run out.

Communications&Media

With easy telephone, mobile and internet access, plus widely available cable-TV, there is no reason not to stay in touch

THE TURKISH TELEPHONE NETWORK is operated by the state monopoly, Türk Telekom. Getting a line is relatively easy and simply involves taking proof of address, your passport and bank details down to the local office. Bills are issued monthly and can be paid in person at your local office or some banks, or from your bank account by direct debit.

Public card phones can be found in most public places, with credit card phones in airports.

MOBILE PHONES

Mobile phone networks are operated by several rival firms, with *Türkcell*, the first and largest company, providing the best coverage. As a foreigner you can have a standard account or a pay-as-you-go line. You can open a standard account at one of the many mobile phone shops in every town, with proof of address in Turkey, your passport and bank details. Bills are paid monthly. Pay-as-you-go lines are even simpler to open, requiring no identification or proof of address, and they are recommended if you are only in the country for short periods of time, or you use the phone very little. On the down side, however, call rates are very high and it can be inconvenient trying to find a card (*hazır kart*) when your credit is finished. Cards are available at mobile phone outlets, corner shops and even some petrol stations.

Handsets are comparatively expensive as their price isn't subsidised by the networks like in the UK. A British handset can be used with a Turkish SIM card only after is has been "unlocked" at a mobile phone shop.

If you intend to use your British mobile phone in Turkey, remember to call your operator to enable international roaming.

THE POST & COURIERS

The Turkish postal service, known as the PTT, has post offices across the country and delivers mail to your door. The service is quite slow and letters may take several days to reach their destination in Turkey, or at least a week to get to the UK. If you have an urgent letter or parcel consider sending in by the APS express service at a small extra charge. Courier companies such as DHL and UPS make international express deliveries, or inside Turkey you can use Aras Kargo, Yurt İçi or one of the other domestic delivery firms for next-day deliveries.

NEWSPAPERS & MAGAZINES

Turkey has a lively press with a wide selection of national, regional and local newspapers. But unless you read Turkish they will be of

THE INTERNET

The internet revolution is in full swing in Turkey, as witnessed by the huge number of internet cafes. Dial-up and ADSL broadband connections are available from Türk Telekom and private internet service providers in the main cities, plus some other areas. Companies like Superonline and E-Kolay offer unlimited dial-up connections from £50 per year and 1 megabyte ADSL broadband from £50 per month, plus a £20 connection charge. You can sign-up online or buy a CD kit at computer and telephone outlets.

TURKISH ISPS
Superonline:
www.superonline.com
E-Kolay:
www.e-kolay.net

Turkey has lots of newspapers, but only one English-language daily, *The Turkish Daily News*.

British, European and some American newspapers are also available from some newsstands in the main cities, airports and tourist areas, though these will be at least a day old

little interest to you. The country does, however, also have an established English-language daily, the *Turkish Daily News*, which includes both domestic and international news stories. British, European and some American newspapers are also available from some newsstands in the main cities, airports and tourist areas, though these will be at least a day old. Magazines such as *Newsweek* and *Time* are also often available.

Cornucopia, an up-market magazine about Turkey, can be found in the largest cities or can be delivered if you take out a subscription. Most international magazines can also be delivered to your home address if you subscribe as an international reader. *Atlas* is a travel magazine, which, although in Turkish, is worth buying for the wonderful photography of the country.

TELEVISION & CABLE TV

Turkey has a huge number of national and local TV stations broadcasting predominantly in Turkish, though several of the state-run TRT channels have a few English language programs.

Türk Telekom offer a cable-TV service in many areas of the country. This is far better for foreign viewers as it includes BBC Prime, CNN, NBC and other European channels.

RADIO

The Turkish airwaves are choked with hundreds of radio stations playing every type of music. In some of the resort areas there are English-language local stations too. It is also possible to pick-up the BBC World Service and Voice of America on short-wave radios, although reception can be patchy. With a broadband internet connection you can listen to a whole host of international radio, probably including your favourite station from back home.

Health, Education & Crime

Excellent value, private healthcare is widely available, though finding a good school can be more difficult in some areas

TURKEY HAS A THREE-TIER HEALTH SYSTEM with state hospitals (*Devlet Hastaneleri*) providing free health care to all Turkish citizens; hospitals that are funded by the equivalent of National Insurance and private clinics and hospitals (*Özel Hastaneleri*). State hospitals vary greatly, but they are often poorly funded, crowded and may not have the most up-to-date equipment. Many staff will not speak English making communication extremely difficult. Having said that, in the event of a serious injury, you will probably receive completely satisfactory treatment in a government hospital. You will be expected to pay for any treatment that you undergo, but medical care is cheap by European standards.

Social Security Hospitals (*SSK Hastaneleri*) are only open to those who have paid into the Turkish social security system, however, conditions are often worse than in the state hospitals.

Standards of care are far better in the private sector, and there are many more English-speaking staff. An increasing number of "medical tourists" are actually travelling from Europe to take advantage of the excellent medical treatment available in Turkey. The cost of treatment is far lower than in the UK, however, you should check with your insurance company before starting any treatment (see below).

In small towns and rural areas government clinics (*Poliklinik*) are often the only source of heathcare. These clinics vary greatly in terms of equipment and standard of care, but are normally perfectly adequate for minor injuries.

Turkish doctors tend to specialise in one particular area of medicine and English-speaking practitioners can be found in most cities and the coastal resorts. Doctor's fees are very reasonable with a standard check-up typically costing £30-£50, which will include a follow-up appointment, if necessary, after 10 days.

HEALTH INSURANCE

Private health insurance for people living abroad is available from UK-based companies such as BUPA. Similar to normal health insurance, international policies have varying levels of cover, with the additional option of repatriation to the UK if you should fall seriously ill. Treatment can be undertaken in any recognised hospital or clinic, but you must check with your insurer that your policy covers the proposed treatment before it gets underway.

Medical insurance schemes are also offered by Turkish companies, such as Axa Oyak. For contact details of firms offering private health insurance see the Directory.

If you travel to Turkey to look for property don't forget to buy travel insurance with sufficient medical cover before you leave.

VACCINATIONS

No special vaccinations are required before you travel to Turkey, although it is a good idea to check that your tetanus and typhoid cover is up-to-date and have a hepatitis A jab. Malaria has made an appearance in recent years in the far south east of the country, but this is a long way from the areas that you are likely to buy property.

LANGUAGE

English is widely spoken in the resort areas, particularly with Turkish people involved in the real estate and tourist industries. Elsewhere, far fewer people speak a foreign language, so it is a good idea to try learning some Turkish. Learning any foreign language requires hard work and perseverance, and Turkish is no different. As a member of the Ural-Altaic language family, which have very little in common with English and Latin-based languages, such as French and Italian, you will have to learn the grammar and a lot of the vocabulary from scratch. On the plus side, Turkish is a phonetic language, so once you have learnt the basic sounds for each of the letters you should be able to pronounce words correctly. There are various self-study books to help you teach yourself Turkish, or you may prefer to enrol in a class at a language school in Turkey (see the Directory). There may even be Turkish evening classes near where you live in the UK.

One of the best ways of learning any language though, is getting out and trying to talk to people. Learn a few simple phrases to practice at the market or in your local shop. And no matter how bad the results are the fact that you are making an effort will really impress most Turkish people. Another good way to learn is to swap lessons with a Turkish person wanting to learn English.

EDUCATION

Turkey's young and rapidly growing population puts immense pressure on the country's education system. Turkish children must complete eight years of compulsory education, but the standard of schooling is often low due to large classes, poor facilities and chronic under-funding. The state school system is divided into Nursery, Primary and Secondary Schools, with students normally attending classes either in the morning or the afternoon. Foreign nationals living in Turkey are entitled to send their children to Turkish state schools, although many choose instead to send them to private or international schools. These generally have much better facilities but are only located in the larger cities, such as Istanbul, Ankara, Izmir and Antalya.

CRIME

Turkey is very safe with crime rates far lower than most European countries, including the UK. You should be wary of pick-pockets in major cities and tourist resorts, but street crime is actually very rare. Property crime is also unusual, but you should take the necessary precautions to secure your apartment or villa, particularly if it is empty for long periods of time. Get to know your neighbours and ask them to keep an eye on things for you. If you are the victim of any kind of crime report the incident immediately to the police, who will file a report that may be necessary for any subsequent insurance claim.

> Turkey is very safe with crime rates far lower than most European countries, including the UK

Food&Shopping

Lunch in a waterside fish restautant near Bodrum

One of the delights of living in Turkey is the fresh, seasonal produce widely available in shops and markets

TURKISH FRUIT AND VEGETABLES are generally far fresher and more tasty than those found in the UK. Particular species come and go with the seasons, rather than being available all year-round. You will also notice that meat is a lot tastier, often because it is truly "free-range". The Turkish staple is bread, although rice and potatoes are also widely eaten. Food retailing has developed rapidly in Turkey in the last decade with large supermarket chains now present in most resorts and towns. As well as a complete range of domestically produced goods - many of which are exported to Europe - supermarkets also stock imported foods, with some familiar British brands available in the coastal resorts. Among the most common supermarkets are *Migros*, *Tansaş* and *Gima*.

Modern shopping malls are a convenient place to shop in cities like Istanbul, Antalya and Izmir, as you can find supermarkets, clothes shops, bookstores and DIY outlets all under one, air-conditioned roof. Smaller shops, known as *bakal*, are found on most street corners in towns and rural areas. They have a smaller choice of produce, usually fresh bread, milk, tinned foods, cigarettes and newspapers. For fruit and vegetables you need to find the local

TONIGHTS
SPECIAL

BALIK
BUĞLAMA
(FISH COOKED
WITH ONIONS,
CARROTS, POTATOES
& HERBS)

THIS IS A
TURKISH
SPECIALITY

The best place to buy fresh produce, and experience local culture at its most colourful, are the weekly markets

greengrocer (*manav*). Most local shops do not accept credit cards and prices are a bit higher than in supermarkets.

The best place to buy fresh produce, and experience local culture at its most colourful, are the weekly markets (*pazar*). These have dozens of stalls selling fresh, seasonal fruit and vegetables, cheeses, meat, fish, olives and nuts. Fun and interesting places to shop, local markets are also the most economical place to buy groceries. Shopping in local shops and markets is a good way to practice any Turkish that you have learnt. Most shop keepers won't speak any English, so a few Turkish words and numbers are very useful.

DINING OUT

Most Turkish resorts and cities have an excellent choice of places to eat these days. Istanbul has many world-class restaurants offering modern dishes prepared to the highest standards. Restaurants serving European-style cuisine, not always terribly well, alongside Turkish dishes are common in the holiday resorts. More traditional options include meat restaurants, called *ocak başı*, where a choice of kebabs, chops and steaks are grilled on open coals. Fish restaurants are also very popular with Turks and foreigners alike, and you can normally select your dinner from a glass-fronted refrigerator. In both types of restaurant you can choose from a huge selection of traditional Turkish starters, known as *meze*. For a quick snack, buffets serving doner kebabs are on most street corners, or the restaurants serving stews, casseroles and soups from stainless steel steam-trays are another good option for lunch.

Furnishing&Importing

There's a wide choice of furniture and electrical equipment available at very reasonable prices but importing is an option too

REMOVAL COMPANIES

If you are shipping furniture to Turkey, it is wise to use a well-established international removal company and a member of the British Association of Removers, see the Directory. Removal firms charge according to the location and the volume of goods to be moved, and will generally send a surveyor around to your home to give you a quote. As a rough guide, the cost of moving furniture from a two-bedroom house to one of the coastal resort is £3,000-£6,000.

CUSTOMS

Anything to do with Turkish customs is notoriously bureaucratic, so you should employ an experienced shipping agent to manage the importation process for you. You can import furniture and household items into Turkey without paying duty provided that you have a valid residence permit. Classed as a "temporary importation", you will need a letter of guarantee from a Turkish bank to leave as a deposit for the unpaid duty. The deposit will be returned to you if you leave the country with the furniture, or if you stay more than five years.

There are also strict rules governing the importation of cars, see page 65. For further information on customs regulations contact the *Turkish Embassy, Tel 020 72456318.*

FURNISHINGS

Good quality furniture and fitted kitchens are available from several nationwide furniture chains, such as *Kelebek* (see the Directory). You can visit one of their showrooms or look at their range on the internet first. Most large towns also have workshops turning out furniture, although the quality may be quite low. Whatever you want, your estate agent will generally point you in the right direction and most items can be delivered within days.

BESPOKE & ANTIQUE FURNITURE

Higher quality bespoke furniture is available in the larger resorts and cities. The Çukurcuma area of Istanbul is particularly famous for its antique shops, but you can also find real and reproduction antique furniture in most of the resorts. Brassware is common and carpets and *kilims* are a real local speciality, which can add lots of character to your Turkish home. Carpet shops also have inexpensive accessories like cushion covers and throws.

ELECTRICAL APPLIANCES

White goods and electrical appliances are manufactured in Turkey, and exported to Europe, by companies such as Beko and Arçelik. These domestic brands are high-quality and much cheaper than imported goods. There are showrooms in most large towns and whatever you buy can be delivered and fitted for a small extra charge

RentingYourProperty

The rental market is only just starting to develop in Turkey, but there is the potential for good returns with the right property

In a crowded rental market choosing the right property is essential for good returns

MOST PEOPLE BUYING in Turkey aim to rent out their property at least some of the year. The promise of solid rental returns on top of strong capital growth has attracted many investors; while those buying primarily for their own use often decide that a few weeks rental can cover the cost of maintaining their property.

Although the Turkish rental market is currently far less developed than countries like France and Spain, there is huge potential for it to grow. Over a million British holidaymakers visit Turkey each year, the vast majority of them booking their flights and accommodation through a travel agent in the UK. The fastest growing sector of this market, however, is independent tourists, who book their flights, accommodation and, perhaps, a hire car separately, often over the internet. Some of these people already decide to rent a villa or apartment, but as the choice and standard of rental accommodation increases, and the cost of airfares drops, so many more will choose to take that option.

At present though, the building boom along the Turkish coast has created a huge pool of rental accommodation, with an over-supply in some areas. This makes it very important that you choose the right location, and the right kind of property, if rental is a primary concern. In resorts such as Alanya, Altınkum and Kuşadası, which are popular with families, apartments on complexes are the easiest to rent, because they are cheaper and have a range of facilities, much like a hotel. In resorts such as Kalkan or Kaş, which attract a wealthier clientele, private villas with pools offer the best rental returns. Wherever you decide to buy, think about the location and who your target market is very carefully. Easy access to the beach and facilities is important for most families renting an apartment, while those choosing a luxury villa will probably prefer a more secluded spot with a glorious sea view. The furniture in a villa should be carefully chosen to add character and atmosphere. In an apartment, the main concerns will be convenience and usability.

The rental season in most of the coastal resorts is from June to the

> Those buying primarily for their own use may decide that a few weeks rental can cover the cost of maintaining their property

A Buyer's Tale
Retiring into Rental

Colin and Carol Andrews decided to buy a holiday home in Turkey after cruising down the coast in a Turkish yacht. "We fell in love with the place," says Colin, who formerly worked as a telecoms engineer. "So we came back for a better look."

Their children were hunting for a house in Spain at the time, so they had a good opportunity to compare what was available in each country. They also paid a brief visit to Greece, before finally deciding to buy in Kaş.

"We felt that Kaş was the right place for us," remembers Carol. "Although we couldn't find a suitable property." Having scoured the area in vain for a three or four-bedroom villa, they decided to buy an off-plan house offered by a local construction company. Situated on the Çukurbağ peninsular, about 5 kilometres from town, the site has wonderful sea views. Importantly, the developer had a proven track record with other well-built villas in the surrounding area. Despite this, Colin and Carol admit to having had some worries.

"We didn't actually get out to see what was going on until the first floor had been constructed," says Colin. "But that made us feel much more relaxed."

A ban on building during the

"We came here to enjoy life, but rental from the villas will provide a useful income."

summer holiday season meant it took two years to complete the villa, by which time the couple were starting to think rather differently about their new holiday home.

"Colin's job was very stressful and our children has moved to Spain by this time," remembers Carol. "So we

decided to move to Turkey permanently, while we were still young enough to enjoy ourselves."

Colin took early retirement and the couple sold-up and drove out to Kaş in August 2004. In the meantime, they'd begun building a second, larger home on an adjacent plot, with a shared investment in a third nearby.

"We certainly never intended to get into property", laughs Colin. "We came out here to enjoy life, but the rental from the villas will provide a useful supplementary income."

Colin and Carol's villa was built by Tandem, www.tandemvillas.com. Visit them at: www.lycian-villas.com

Rental potential is best in an area with plenty to see and do.

beginning of October, with the summer and autumn half-term holidays, along with July and August, the busiest times. A well chosen rental property, which is marketed successfully, should be occupied for 12-14 weeks a year. However in some resorts, namely Alanya, demand is developing for rental properties in the off-season, as a growing number of retirees look to escape the northern European winter. Winter lets, although at a lower rate, significantly boost annual rental returns. In the larger cities like Istanbul and Antalya, the rental market is much more established and year-round.

As part of the area guides in this book we give an assessment of rental potential and typical rates that are charged.

Wherever your rental property, successful marketing and management is of key importance to achieving successful returns. Many estate agents and independent companies offer management services, which include cleaning, laundry services, airport pick-ups, maintenance and welcome baskets. Some are also marketing the properties through UK travel agents or their own websites. This is very convenient if you are not around to look after things yourself. The fee for these services is typically 15-20% of the rental income.

Several UK travel companies who specialise in Turkish villa holidays, such as Tapestry, Exclusive Escapes and Cachet Travel, market suitable properties, paying the owner a percentage of the rental income. Owners must normally sign a contract for at least 3 years and they can reserve several weeks for their own use each season.

Lastly, lots of people choose the DIY approach, advertising their villa or apartment in the classified section of a local newspaper, or on one of the rental websites that are springing up. Alternatively, they may rely on friends, family and colleagues to spread the word.

If you decide to take this route it is wise to prepare a website and some simple promotional material, including photos of the property and rates. You will also have to organise for someone to see guests in and clean up after they have left, if you are not around yourself.

> In the larger cities like Istanbul and Antalya, the rental market is much more established and year-round

The Aegean

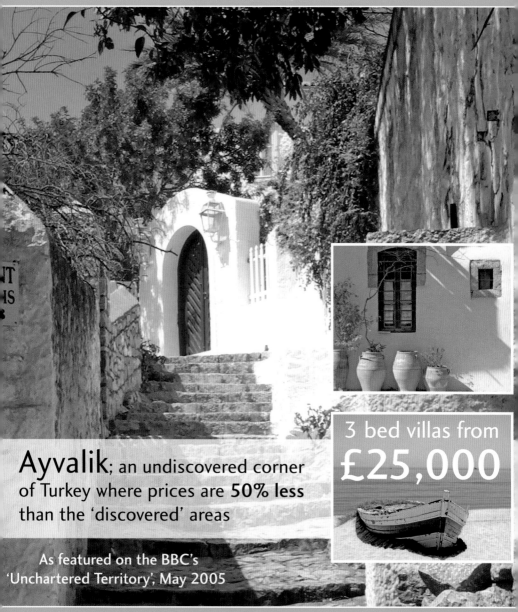

Ayvalık

In Ottoman days the town had a wealthy Greek population, whose grand town houses make great renovation projects today

ON THE AEGEAN COAST NORTH OF IZMIR, Ayvalık is surrounded by countryside carpeted with olive-groves. Famous for olive oil and soap, the town had a large Greek population until 1923 and their memory lives on in the atmospheric old quarter with its impressive civic architecture and churches, which now function as mosques. Built by Greek merchants and businessmen at the turn of the last century, some of the grand stone town houses have been renovated in the last 15 years, although many more stand in various stages of disrepair. Across the bay from the town, and reached by a narrow causeway or small ferry, is the island of Alibey, where there are more Ottoman Greek houses and some excellent fish restaurants. There is a beach at the small resort of Sarımsaklı, 5 km south of Ayvalık town, while in the town centre restaurants overlook the water and there is a busy high-street of shops. A yacht marina has been built on the edge of town and there is a ferry service to the Greek island of Lesbos in the summer.

The Greek houses of the old town and Alibey make excellent renovation projects. All are now protected by strict planning controls. However, many are in an advanced state of decay and virtually need rebuilding. Bare in mind that access to some of the houses is difficult as many of the cobbled streets in the old town are too narrow for modern vehicles. Instead, building materials are delivered, and builders rubbish taken away, by horse-drawn carts.

There are cooperatives and some new villa developments on the island of Alibey, as well as in the suburb of Çamlık and Sarımsaklı. Many of the houses on the cooperative developments are poor quality and would need renovating. Prices start from about £30,000 for a small villa on an established cooperative. Expect to pay upwards of £65,000 for a newer, higher quality villa, with some sea front houses on Alibey fetching over £100,000.

Prices for the old Greek houses in the town center and on Alibey vary hugely depending on the condition of the building and its location. A typical price for a large four-bedroom house in need of extensive renovation, but no major structural work, is £70,000. Make sure you get a builder and an architect to examine the building carefully and give you an estimate for the conversion costs before buying.

Off-the-beaten-track for European tourists, the potential for holiday lets is currently poor. The area is, however, popular with domestic tourists from Istanbul and elsewhere.

AYVALIK AT A GLANCE
Population: 27,000
Telephone Area Code: 0266
Airport: Izmir (2.5 hours)
Tourist Information:
Yat Limanı Karşısı
Tel: 0266 312 2122

PROPERTY LOWDOWN
TYPICAL PRICES:
Apartment (2-bed): £30,000
Villa (3-bed): £55,000
Rental Potential: Poor
Advantages: Atmospheric
Turkish town. Many old houses.
Disadvantages: Far from Izmir
airport. Poor rental potential.

ESTATE AGENTS
Ayvalık Property:
Tel: 01622-764200,
www.ayvalikproperty.com

In need of TLC: One of Ayvalık's dilapidated Greek houses

Çeşme

Mostly ignored by foreign buyers, Çeşme attracts Turkish tourists and second home owners with its beaches, dining and nightlife

ÇEŞME AT A GLANCE
Population: 37,372
Telephone Area Code: 0232
Airport: Izmir (1 hour)
Tourist Information:
Iskele Meydanı No 8
Tel: 0232 7126653

PROPERTY LOWDOWN
TYPICAL PRICES:
Apartment (2-bed): £45,000
Villa (3-bed): £110,000
Rental Potential: Good
Advantages: Close to Izmir airport. Good beaches and windsurfing. An excellent selection of property
Disadvantages:
Expensive in parts. Some areas are over-developed.

ESTATE AGENTS
Villas in Turkey:
Tel: 0232 7122326
www.villasinturkey.net

Ilıca's fine white sand beach

OVERLOOKING THE GREEK ISLAND OF CHIOS, Çeşme is a small Turkish holiday town. Only a 45-minute drive from the city of Izmir, many Turkish families have second homes in the area. In recent years the town has also become a fashionable summer destination for young people from Istanbul and Ankara. Despite its domestic appeal, comparatively few foreign tourists visit or buy property.

In the town itself, a large Genoese castle stands guard over the harbour, from where car ferries leave for Chios and ports in Italy. The suburb of Ilıca, 5 km east of the town center, has the area's best beach, while nearby Alaçatı, formerly a small village of Greek houses, which is now surrounded by villa developments, is popular with windsurfers from across Europe. There are several large marinas in the area, as well as a hot spring and thermal centre.

To the south of the main town, there are more beaches beyond the fishing village of Çiftlikköy, which is a pleasant year-round Turkish community with a scenic seaside position. In the opposite direction, Dalyanköy has a small harbour surrounded by fish restaurants and overlooked by villa developments. The local dining is varied and the nightlife is lively during the summer months. Without a car, access between Çeşme's various resorts is simple with regular minibus services.

Property prices are generally higher than other Turkish resorts due to strong domestic demand and strict planning controls. However, there is a very good choice of properties available with apartments and villas to suit all budgets and tastes.

Places in the centre of Çeşme benefit from easy access to restaurants, bars and shopping, although it is very busy and congested in summer. Prices in the town start from £36,000 for a two-bedroom apartment, or from £65,000 for a larger apartment with views of the harbour or castle.

In Dalyanköy and Çiftlikköy new three-bedroom villas with sea views are available from £100,000, with older resale properties considerably cheaper. The property in Ilıca and nearby Paşalimanı is more expensive. Expect to pay upwards of £200,000, and often a lot more, for a villa with its own garden and pool. These areas have good access to the beach, but Ilıca itself is crowded in summer.

Prices in Alaçatı are more reasonable, with a choice of renovated houses in the village, or villas on complexes typically starting from £90,000. A short drive from the beach and a new marina, the properties in Alaçatı don't have sea views.

The rental potential for villas is particularly good in Çeşme thanks to the area's popularity with domestic tourists. The market is divided between seasonal summer rentals, mostly to families from nearby Izmir, and shorter holiday lets to expatriate Turks and foreigners.

Kuşadası

The town has grown explosively in the last decade, becoming a major package holiday destination and property hot-spot

ONCE A SMALL AEGEAN FISHING TOWN, in the last 20 years Kuşadası has grown into a major resort popular with British and Irish package tourists and domestic holidaymakers. The town is also a port-of-call for cruise liners, whose passengers disembark to visit the nearby archaeological site of Ephesus, which is one of Turkey's biggest tourist attractions. There are many other interesting sights nearby, and the Dilek National Park, 30 km south, has good beaches and forest walks.

The town centre is bustling year-round and there is a good selection of shops and services, including several large supermarkets. The narrow streets of the old town are lined with touristy shops, restaurants, bars and clubs, which are crowded during the summer season. There is a large marina and beaches just north and south of the center, where many of the largest hotel complexes and villa developments are situated. Kadınlar Denizi (Ladies' Beach), to the south of the center, is the town's best-known beach.

Kuşadası has experienced explosive growth in recent years. Although the new apartments and villas are primarily for the Turkish market, the number of foreign buyers has increased rapidly to over 3,500. Poorly planned, low-quality developments have spoilt some areas. However, on the plus side there is a huge variety of property to choose from and prices are low.

Apartments predominate in the centre but there are also some older villas. These properties benefit from being close to the amenities and shopping of the town centre, but they may be noisy depending on their location. Prices start from £25,000 for a very basic two-bedroom apartment. A short walk or minibus ride from the center, prices are considerably higher in the Ladies' Beach area, particularly if you want a view of the sea. Expect to pay from £60,000 for a new two-bedroom apartment near the beach.

South of the town, Long Beach and Davutlar have beaches backed by orchards and agricultural land. There are also some huge, ugly cooperative developments. It is a much quieter area with only small shops for basic supplies, although minibuses into Kuşadası run every few minutes during the season. Prices are lower than in town, with a new-build villa on a complex with shared pool typically starting from £40,000.

To the north of Kuşadası and closer to Izmir airport, the small Turkish resort of Özdere offers excellent value for money.

Property prices have risen rapidly over the last few years due to strong demand from domestic and foreign buyers. The resulting building boom has produced a glut of rental properties. However, rental opportunities are best in the most desirable areas of town such as Ladies' Beach.

KUŞADASI AT A GLANCE

Population: 60,000
Telephone Area Code: 0256
Airport: Izmir (45 mins)
Tourist Information:
Iskele Meydanı
Tel: 0256 614 1103

PROPERTY LOWDOWN
TYPICAL PRICES:

Apartment (2-bed): £35,000
Villa (3-bed): £65,000
Rental Potential: Fair
Advantages:
Close to Izmir airport.
Good year-round facilities and services. Close to tourist attractions and beaches
Disadvantages:
Unsightly development in parts.
Shorter season than further south

ESTATE AGENTS
Expert Real Estate
Tel 0256 6131770
www.turkeyexpert.co.uk

Kuşadası is one of the largest resorts on the Aegean coast

turkish
connextions.co.uk

Want the property of your dreams on the Aegean Coast?
Contact the UK's leading specialists Prices from £29,000

Altınkum

With its sandy beach and affordable property, Altınkum is one of the most popular places for British buyers

ALTINKUM IS A LARGE PACKAGE RESORT with a series of sandy beaches that give it its name – "Golden Sand"- in Turkish. Popular with British and domestic holidaymakers, the town's pedestrianised seafront promenade is lined with restaurants and bars. During the summer months there are a variety of water sports and leisure facilities on the beach, which is gently sloping and ideal for children. Didyma's famous Temple of Apollo is within the town itself, with the ancient Greek city of Miletus and several other archaeological sites close by.

At the moment Altınkum is a 90-minute drive from Bodrum airport. A new coastal road, due for completion in 2006, will cut this journey to an hour. The town has a new public hospital, which can provide basic healthcare, with larger private hospitals in Bodrum and Kuşadası. Shopping facilities are good with several large supermarkets and a weekly market for fresh produce.

Altınkum is popular with both domestic and British buyers. There are currently over 3,000 foreign-owned properties in the area, with most being used as holiday homes by British families. The town has a wide choice of property at the mid and lower end of the market, with about 75% of the housing stock made up of apartments. Very basic two-bedroom apartments generally start from around £30,000. New-build and off-plan apartments are often on complexes with excellent facilities.

Away from the center there are more villa developments, with areas such as Çamlık and Aytepe offering quieter surroundings, yet only a short walk or minibus ride from the main beach and shopping. Near the site of a planned marina, Aytepe has seen rapid development and major price increases in the last year. A new three-bedroom villa on a complex with shared pool typically sells from £60,000-£70,000.

The smaller resort of Akbük, situated 10 km south of Altınkum on a wide bay backed by mountains, has become popular with buyers wanting more peaceful surroundings. The area has resale and new-build villas and represents excellent value for money at the moment. A three-bedroom villa with pool starts from £55,000 and land with building permission is also available.

Infrastructural development has struggled to keep pace with building in some areas of Altınkum. Many access roads are unsurfaced and become muddy or even impassable during the winter. There are also problems with drainage in low-lying areas.

Rental potential should be excellent thanks to Altınkum's popularity with British package tourists. However, the on-going building boom has created a large stock of rental properties, which makes choosing the right property very important.

ALTINKUM AT A GLANCE
Population: 30,000
Telephone Area Code: 0256
Airport: Bodrum (1.5 hours)
Tourist Information:
Iskele Meydanı
Tel: 0256 614 1103

PROPERTY LOWDOWN
TYPICAL PRICES:
Apartment (3-bed): £35,000
Villa (3-bed): £65,000
Rental Potential: Fair
Advantages: Easy airport access. Good beach. Affordable property
Disadvantages: Crowded during the summer. Poor infrastructure in some areas.

ESTATE AGENTS:
Turkish Homes: Tel 0256 8133460
www.turkish-homes.com
Turkish Connextions:
Tel 01772 735151 (UK)
www.turkishconnextions.co.uk

The Temple of Apollo was famous in ancient times for its Oracle

TURKISH HOMES

Dream Properties at Dream Prices

Turkish Homes is a leading estate agent, selling and renting property throughout Turkey.

Visit our website, www.turkish-homes.com, for the largest portfolio of properties available.

Whether you are looking for a £30,000 apartment or £150,000 villa, we will help you find exactly what you are looking for.

If you come to Turkey, why not visit one of our offices and meet the team? We have branches across the Bodrum peninsular resorts, and in Altinkum and Kusadasi.

We are always happy to help and offer advice on the Turkish property purchasing process.

www.turkish-homes.com

Contact us on tel: +44 (0) 845 331 2644 (UK), +90 (0) 256 813 3460 (Turkey)
email: info@turkish-homes.com

Bodrum

Ancient Halicarnassus is now Turkey's most sophisticated resort, with a wide range of property and its own airport

BODRUM IS ONE OF TURKEY'S most established and cosmopolitan coastal resorts. Originally a small fishing centre built in the shadow of a magnificent Crusader castle, Bodrum has a history stretching back 2,000 years, when it was the capital of the tyrant Mausolus and home to his tomb, one of the 'Seven Wonders of the World'. More recently the town was a bohemian retreat for Turkish artists and intellectuals. In the last two decades it has grown massively, becoming a destination for package holidaymakers and domestic tourists, but also the elite of Turkish society. Renowned for its bars and nightlife, the town also boasts good restaurants and a museum housed in the restored Castle of St John. There is a large harbour and a fully equipped marina, with ferries to the Greek island of Kos. Beyond the town itself, the 700 km2 Bodrum peninsular is ringed by a series of smaller, quite distinct resorts.

Local healthcare provisions are excellent with several well-equipped private hospitals. Shopping in Bodrum is also good with a choice of large supermarkets and a weekly market for fresh produce. Shopping facilities are more limited in the smaller resorts.

The Bodrum peninsular is very popular with Turkish second home owners. This means that there is considerable competition for desirable properties and prices are high in areas that are favoured by the Turkish jet set. It also means that there is an excellent choice of property. Local restrictions limit buildings to three stories across the entire peninsular.

Bodrum town is dominated by resale houses, which typically sell for upwards of £130,000. The top-end villas, in scenic positions overlooking the castle, sell for millions of pounds. Mostly owned by Turkish families, Bodrum's more modest houses are often sold by word-of-mouth and are difficult to find. Two-bedroom apartments typically sell from £50,000.

Several kilometres west of the centre, Gümbet developed as an overflow, but is now a resort in its own right. Favoured by British package tourists, property prices are lower than Bodrum, with a two-bedroom apartment selling from £45,000, and a three-bedroom house from £55,000. Many areas are noisy in the season and most local businesses shut in winter.

Large parts of Turgutreis, at the west end of the peninsular, are off-limits to foreign buyers due to its status as a military zone. However, the town has a new marina and is popular with package holidaymakers, particularly from Britain.

The area around Gümüşlük has become popular in

BODRUM AT A GLANCE
Population: 35,000
Telephone Area Code: 0252
Airport: Bodrum (25 mins)
Tourist Information:
Barış Meydanı
Tel: 0252 3161091

There is considerable competition for desirable properties and prices are high in areas that are favoured by the Turkish jet set

PROPERTY LOWDOWN
TYPICAL PRICES
Apartment (2-bed): £55,000
Villa (3-bed): £95,000
Rental Potential: Good
Advantages: Easy access from
the UK in summer. Good
restaurants, nightlife and facilities.
Wide variety of property
Disadvantages:
Crowded in the summer
High prices in some areas
Poor infrastructure in parts

LOCAL AGENTS
Turkish Homes:
Tel (UK) 0845 3312644
www.turkish-homes.com
Cumberland Properties:
Tel (UK) 020 74358113
www.cumberland-properties.com

recent years. The village itself is several kilometres inland from a small bay, with a row of excellent fish restaurants and a pretty beach. Property in the village is all resale, with some renovated stone cottages and larger villas starting from £100,000. Development in the beach area is strictly controlled due to the archaeological remains of ancient Mindos, and property is hard to come by. However, there is large-scale development along the coast towards Yalıkavak. The area lacks infrastructure and access is poor, but there is a good choice of villa developments, with prices typically starting from £55,000 for a small three-bedroom semi-detached villa on a complex.

On the north coast, Yalıkavak has a wide cross-section of property from apartments and small villa complexes, to luxury mansions. The village itself has a new marina and waterfront promenade. Similar to Gümüşlük, some property sold as being in "Yalıkavak" may be a long way from the centre, with no public transport.

Göltürkbükü is the place to be for wealthy and aspiring Turks. Favoured by the high society of Istanbul and Ankara, local property prices have rocketed. Despite this, the local infrastructure is poorly developed and shopping is limited. There are fewer foreign buyers in this area.

Rental potential is good in Bodrum and the larger resorts of the peninsular. Weekly holiday lets start from £250-£300 per week for a two-bed apartment and £500 for a villa. There is also demand for longer-term lets from domestic tourists.

Expert View
What's so special about Bodrum?

The Bodrum peninsula has everything and more. It is an internationally recognised name with a well developed infrastructure and its own airport. It is historically rich and has the geography to offer spectacular views from many properties. There is an excellent choice of restaurants and shops, plus the town itself doesn't shut down in winter because of the large local population.

Is it still a good investment?
In short, yes. Property prices have rocketed over the last couple of years and are showing no signs of

Clair Tatlıcı, Managing Director, Turkish Homes, www.turkish-homes.com

slowing down thanks to strong domestic and overseas demand. Also, new amenities will greatly change the market. There are currently two golf courses planned in the area, which will only

increase Bodrum's popularity.

Where is the best place to buy?
I see big potential in the area between Yalıkavak and Gümüslük. Development there is intense and competition is high, which is keeping a stable control on prices, but ensures that standards are high enough to make little difference if a property is new or a couple of years old. With the level of new construction ensuring that there is lots of choice for the foreign market, it will only be a short time before the services that these buyers demand are in place.

A Buyer's Tale
A Piece of Paradise

April and her husband, Michael, had a very clear idea of what they wanted as a summer home. "We were looking for a stone house near the sea," remembers April. "Oh, and it needed olive trees in the garden."

Having looked in Italy and Spain, they decided to search for their dream villa in Turkey. As frequent visitors to the country, they appreciated the relaxed way of life and unspoilt scenery. "We always felt welcome in Turkey as the people are so friendly," says April. "Of course, the prices were reasonable in comparison to other countries we'd looked in too." Another important consideration for the couple was accessibility. With it's airport served by regular flights from the UK, Bodrum was a natural place to start looking. The couple also appreciated the area's cosmopolitan atmosphere, with enough Turkish and foreign home-owners to create an interesting community with good services. Once they'd decided on the area, finding the right villa was relatively easy. They flew to Bodrum for a weekend and were shown 30 properties by a local estate agent.

"There was lots to choose from," says April. "With prices varying from £30,000 for a tiny box to £300,000 for a luxury

The pretty harbour and restautants of Gümüşlük are a short drive from the villa.

> With its airport served by regular flights from the UK, Bodrum was a natural place to start looking

palace."

They opted for a two-bedroom villa on a small development with shared pool. Near the village of Gündoğan and the up-and-coming resort of Yalıkavak, it is about 20 minutes drive from Bodrum.

"It's perfect," says April. "Remote enough to get-away from it all; yet convenient for the airport and Bodrum town." On the market for £45,000, the house is built of stone and has a wonderful sea view. Part of a development of nine properties, they have a communal pool and a caretaker to look after things. "It was important to have someone to look after the house," says April. "As we only visit for holidays and the place is empty the rest of the time."

Quality Living in Bodrum
with Cagdas Group

With sun-soaked beaches and the bluest waters of the Aegean, relaxed during the day, vibrant at night, Bodrum has become one of the hottest spots in the eastern Mediterranean...

Now, you can own a beautiful house in the best areas of Bodrum offered by Cagdas Properties, a subsidiary organization of Cagdas Group, the leading developer and builder of quality homes. We have on offer various off-plan projects and a wide range of homes with different specifications, sizes and locations to choose from.

For further information please visit
www.cagdasproperties.com

West Mediterranean

Marmaris

One of Turkey's largest resorts, Marmaris has beaches, water sports and lots of night-life, plus a good choice of property too

MARMARIS SITS ON A WIDE BAY protected by steep pine-forested mountains. Sultan Süleyman the Magnificent built the town's tiny castle before invading Rhodes in 1522, but little else remains of the quiet fishing town of yesteryear. Modern Marmaris is a large urban centre and one of Turkey's major resorts, receiving over one million visitors last year. Not surprisingly it boasts excellent services, entertainment and shopping, as well as several large marinas, including the 750-berth Netsel Marina - one of the largest in the eastern Mediterranean. Marmaris is surrounded by beautiful countryside with plenty of options for excursions. Although the beaches in the town itself aren't good, the nearby suburb of İçmeler has a stretch of sandy beach with water sports and other activities available throughout the season. İçmeler's promenade is backed by large resort hotels, behind which are a grid of touristy shops, restaurants, villas and apartments blocks. In contrast to other areas of the town, the suburb is neat with good roads, carefully kept communal gardens and a well-developed infrastructure

Enclosed by steep mountains, there is very little new land available for development in Marmaris. Prices look set to continue rising in the face of strong demand from both domestic and foreign buyers.

The town centre is dominated by re-sale apartments many of which are over 5 years old. Conveniently close to the main concentration of restaurants, shopping and nightlife, basic two-bedroom apartments in this area typically sell from £30,000.

The suburb of Armutalan is popular with wealthy Turkish buyers and counts the former Turkish president Kenan Evren as one of its seasonal residents. The area has a mix of villas and apartment complexes with prices for a three-bedroom apartment starting from £60,000, and a newly built four-bedroom house with a pool typically selling for upwards of £140,000. North east of Marmaris, the new suburb of Beldibi has cheaper property and good transport links to the centre. Closer to the seafront, Siteler has a number of new developments, with apartments ranging from £55,000-£120,000 depending on size, facilities and location.

Prices in İçmeler are higher due to strong demand from both foreign and local buyers. Expect to pay over £140,000 for a new three-bedroom villa, and over £95,000 for a two-bedroom apartment on a new complex. Cheaper re-sale properties are often available, though they may need extensive modernization. With easy access to the beach, rental potential is highest in İçmeler.

MARMARIS AT A GLANCE
Population: 58,000
Telephone Area Code: 0252
Airport: 1.5 hours (Dalaman)
Tourist Information:
İskele Meydanı No 2
Tel 0252 412 1035

PROPERTY LOWDOWN
TYPICAL PRICES:
Apartment (2-bed): £40,000
Villa (3-bed): £145,000
Rental Potential: Fair-Good
Advantages:
Varied entertainment and leisure activities. Excellent healthcare and services
Disadvantages:
Poor infrastructure in some areas. Limited availability of property

ESTATE AGENTS
Cartier Real Estate:
Tel 0252 4552979
www.icmelerestateagency.com
Red Tek Real Estate:
Tel (UK) 0870 7779098
www.redtekrealestate.com

Datça

An isolated backwater until recently, the resort is still relatively unknown by European tourists and property-hunters

ON THE SCENIC REŞADIYE PENINSULAR, Datça is a small town built around a pretty harbour. Bad road access from Marmaris, 75 km east, gave it a feeling of isolation and slowed development until fairly recently. The area is a popular holiday venue for Turkish families, many of whom own second homes in the area. The local population quadruples in summer, to about 45,000. Datca's harbour is a popular port-of-call for yachts and several local beaches have been given the coveted Blue Flag award. Work to widen and improve the highway east is largely complete and there is a car-ferry from Bodrum in summer. Local shops stock all the essentials, though luxuries and imported goods must be bought from Marmaris. Most of the area's properties have been built for the Turkish market and may need renovation. Prices range from £35,000- over £75,000 for a detached villa with garden. In the centre of town, basic re-sale apartments are available from £30,000, with new builds from £50,000. Local developers have started targeting foreign property buyers with new apartment complexes. Largely unknown to European holidaymakers, rental potential is poor at present.

DATÇA AT A GLANCE
Population: 8,800
Telephone Area Code: 0252
Airport: Dalaman (2.5 hours)
Tourist Information:
Hukumet Binasi, Iskele Mah.
Tel 0252 712 3163

PROPERTY LOWDOWN
Typical Prices:
Apartment (2-bed): £40,000
Villa (3-bed): £75,000
Rental Potential: Poor

ESTATE AGENTS
Avatar International:
Tel (UK) 0870 7282827
www.avatar-turkey.com

Dalaman, Dalyan & Göcek

A beautiful area, great for nature lovers, with goverment investment set to improve the infrastructure and facilities

DALAMAN AREA AT A GLANCE
Population: 17,600
Telephone Area Code: 0252
Airport: 5-30 mins (Dalaman)
Tourist Information:
Dalaman Airport Terminal
Tel 0252 7925220

PROPERTY LOWDOWN
TYPICAL PRICES:
Apartment (2-bed): £50,000
Villa (3-bed): £70,000
Rental Potential: Fair
Advantages: Close to airport.
Excellent beaches and activities.
New infrastructural developments
Disadvantages: Limited services
and amenities in some areas.
Quiet in winter.

ESTATE AGENTS
Curbano ğlu
Tel (UK) 0871 7113919
www.curbanoglu.com
Dalaman Estates
Tel 0252 6923561
www.dalamanestates.co.uk

TRADITIONALLY AN AGRICULTURAL AREA, growing citrus, vegetables and cotton, Dalaman was put on the tourist map by its international airport. As one of the south coast's gateways, hundreds of thousands of tourists pass through each season, although comparatively few stay. Dalaman itself is a work-a-day Turkish market town sprawling across a flat plain. Although not particularly picturesque, it offers a slice of real Turkish life. To the south of the town, a cluster of luxury hotels sit on a beautiful Blue Flag-awarded beach at Sarıgerme. But there are few other facilities beyond the hotels at present. Nearby Dalyan (pop. 4,000), nestling in a pretty location beside a winding river, is a small resort catering for British and European tourists. Local attractions include an excellent beach at Iztuzu, thermal mud baths and the ruins of ancient Kaunos. The area as a whole offers unspoilt rural countryside, with white water rafting and excellent bird-watching.

The government's decision to channel investment into the area's infrastructure as part of an ambitious tourism development project has encouraged intense interest from developers. The effect on prices has been dramatic even by Turkish standards, with the cost of land more than doubling in a year. Although these huge increases have slowed, plans for a new golf course and several marinas in the area, and a road tunnel cutting journey times to Göcek, make the area attractive for investors and holiday home buyers. The small resort of Göcek, tucked at the head of a narrow bay, is an important yachting center with four marinas, including the upmarket Port Göcek.

Dalaman has a mix of older re-sale houses and apartments, new-builds and off-plan developments. Most new developments are apartment complexes, although new-build villas are also available. Villas range from £55,000, with a new three-bedroom detached house selling from £65,000. Apartments start from £45,000 for a three-bedroom, new-build on a complex with shared pool. Expect to pay at least £15,000 more for a similar property in Sarıgerme due to its proximity to the beach.

The choice of property is more limited in Dalyan and Göcek, and prices are higher. Three bedroom villas typically sell for £95,000-£130,000 in Dalyan depending on the location. In Göcek, a similar size property with a view is currently worth £140,000-£200,000. The rental market is undeveloped in Dalaman, though holiday lets are possible in Dalyan and Göcek.

A Buyer's Tale
Dalaman Dreams

Jenny Jones and Neville Horton visited Turkey for a fortnight in April 2004 to look for a holiday home around Fethiye. Not finding anything suitable within their budget, they decided to try nearby Dalaman. "You get a lot more for your money in Dalaman," says Jenny. "And we've come to really like the area." Primarily an agricultural town, they both like the laid-back atmosphere and the fact that it isn't very touristy. Being so close to the airport is also a bonus. The couple looked at two properties in Dalaman before deciding on a three-bedroom, two-bathroom house being sold by a local family. Within their budget of £30,000, the house ticked all the right boxes, being large enough to accommodate friends and family and with enough space in the garden for a pool. It also had lots of character, although the 8 year-old building was in need of extensive modernisation. The couple had a local builder give them a quote for the alterations. He also checked the structure, giving it a clean bill of health. Shortly after completing in June, they began by replacing the window frames, which were rotten, with double-glazing. They also added a new bathroom on the ground floor having discovered that the existing toilet wasn't connected to the main drains. "We had some very funny and frustrating times with the builders," remembers Jenny. "Mostly down to misunderstandings

Jenny and Neville bought from Dalaman Estates, www.dalamanestates.co.uk

"It became harder and harder for us to leave each time we visited"

and lack of communication." Although the work was meant to be supervised by a foreman, they quickly discovered how important it was to be there themselves, to make sure things got done the

way they wanted. "Unfortunately, the standard of work is far lower than in the UK," says Jenny. "But you have to accept that and get on with it." Everything was finally finished in January 2005, by which time they liked Dalaman so much, that they were toying with the idea of living there permanently. "It became harder for us to leave each time we visited," explains Jenny. "We love the relaxed lifestyle and we've made good friends." Both self-employed, Jenny as an alternative therapist and Neville as a tattoo artist, they are still thinking about selling-up in England and moving out to Turkey.

Fethiye,Çalış,Ovacik&Hisarönü

Good beaches, leisure options and services, plus a large choice of property, make Fethiye one of the most popular areas

FETHIYE AREA AT A GLANCE
Population: 60,000
Telephone Area Code: 0252
Airport: Dalaman (45 mins)
Tourist Information:
Iskele Karşısı 1
Tel 0252 6141527

PROPERTY LOWDOWN
Typical Prices:
Apartment (2-bed): £45,000
Villa (3-bed): £110,000
Rental Potential: Fair
Advantages: Close to airport.
Year-round facilities and services in Fethiye. Good beaches and tourist attractions
Disadvantages: Urban setting in Fethiye may put off some buyers. Rental potential reduced for the same reason.
Resort areas quiet in winter.

ESTATE AGENTS
Hanel Houses: Tel 0252 6148810
www.hanelhouse.com
Lagoon Estates: Tel 0252 6129193
www.lagoonestates.com
Taurean Properties:
Tel 0252 6132377
www.taureanproperties.co.uk

SITTING ON A WIDE BAY backed by mountains, Fethiye is a bustling market town at the heart of one the country's most popular areas for foreign buyers. As the administrative center for the nearby resorts of Ölüdeniz, Ovacik/Hisarönü and Çalış, the local economy is dominated by tourism, although few tourists stay in the town itself. Fethiye is an important stop for coastal cruises and the existing harbour facilities were joined in 2004 by the 400-berth Ece Saray Marina. The town has a pleasant atmosphere and thanks to a large local population shops and services stay open year-round.

Inland from a waterside promenade is a lively bazaar district, known as Paspatur. Other tourist attractions include an amphitheatre and several Lycian tombs. Shopping is good with large supermarkets and a huge weekly market for fresh produce. There are two modern hospitals with English-speaking staff.

Fethiye is close to tourist attractions, such as the Saklıkent gorge and ancient Xanthos. The beaches at Ölüdeniz and Çalış (see below) are even nearer with regular minibus services to both.

Modern apartments dominate the town, with many built for local people and Turkish second home owners. Due to a major earthquake in 1957, very few old buildings remain. To the west of the center, Karagözler is a quiet residential district overlooking the bay. Apart from a few old houses most of the villas and small apartment buildings were built in the last 20 years. Many have superb views and thanks to the area's popularity, prices are high. Expect to pay from £135,000 for a three-bedroom house, although a nice villa with garden can fetch over £180,000. Elsewhere in town, three-bedroom apartments range from £35,000 to over £60,000 depending on the location and quality of build. Many older apartments were built for the domestic market and also may not meet current building regulations. Taşyaka and Deliktaş are popular residential areas to the east of the centre. Both have a choice of new-build villas and apartment complexes, with easy access to Ölüdeniz and Çalış. Prices start from £40,000 for a two-bedroom apartment. Prices in all areas have risen steadily with annual increases of at least 15%.

Fethiye has a good long-term rental market, but many holiday renters prefer to be in the beach resorts, rather than a bus ride away.

The beach resort of Çalış, 5 km north of Fethiye, has grown-up along a waterfront promenade lined with hotels and apartments. Popular with British package tourists, the resort now has a large community of permanent British residents

and holiday home owners. There's a good selection of restaurants and bars locally, though many close for the winter. However, minibuses and water-taxis give easy access to Fethiye town centre, just 10 minutes away. Water sports and excursions are available from the beach in season.

Çalış has expanded rapidly in recent years with development creeping several kilometres inland from the sea. There is a mix of new-build, off-plan and re-sale villas and apartments available. Many of the newer apartments are on complexes, often with shared facilities, while older properties may need renovating. Prices vary according to location with a premium paid for villas or apartments nearer the beach. Apartments start from about £35,000, although prices for a nice two-bedroom unit on a complex with shared pool usually start from £50,000. Villa prices vary from £75,000 to over £130,000 depending on the build quality, facilities and distance to the beach. Land for building is limited, although plots do occasionally come onto the market.

Çalış is a popular holiday resort so rental potential is good, with weekly rates of £250-£300 for a two-bedroom apartment with shared pool; £750-£1,000 for a four-bedroom villa with private pool.

Nestling on a plateau surrounded by forested mountains, 8km south of Fethiye, Hisarönü and Ovacik have become very popular property spots. Strict building controls and a lack of flat land around the picturesque Ölüdeniz lagoon, 4 km south, encouraged development in these neighbouring villages, transforming them into resorts in their own right. They now have hotels, shops, restaurants and bars, though many local businesses close for the winter. The scenic setting and easy access to Ölüdeniz beach and Fethiye have attracted a large number of foreign, mainly British, buyers.

Hisarönü and Ovacik have a good selection of new-build apartments and off-plan developments, although high demand has pushed prices up dramatically. A new three-bedroom apartment on a complex with shared pool typically starts from £65,000, with three-bedroom villas with private pool ranging from £125,000 to over £200,000. Prices increase significantly on the slopes above the main road in Ovacik, where most properties benefit from excellent views.

Rental potential in Ovacik and Hisarönü is good with weekly rates of over £1,000 for a 3-4 bedroom villa with garden and pool.

The nearby village of Kayaköyü, clustered beneath a deserted town abandoned in 1923 by its Greek inhabitants, has some stone houses set in beautiful rural surroundings. However, due to the area's protected status proceed with caution and make sure that a Turkish solicitor undertakes thorough searches before buying.

ÇALIŞ PROPERTY LOWDOWN
TYPICAL PRICES:
Apartment (2-bed): £47,000
Villa (3-bed): £85,000
Rental Potential: Good

HISARÖNÜ & OVACIK
PROPERTY LOWDOWN
TYPICAL PRICES:
Apartment (2-bed): £57,000
Villa (3-bed): £135,000
Rental Potential: Good

The scenic setting and easy access to Ölüdeniz beach and Fethiye have attracted a large number of foreign, mainly British, buyers

A Buyer's Tale
Buying in Çaliş

John and Patricia Hulme had only been married a few months when they decided they would like to start a new life in the sun. "We had both got to the stage where we were simply working to live in the UK," says John, who was a fireman in Preston for 20 years. "Rather than enjoying ourselves."

Both John and Patricia had grown-up children and aged parents, so they didn't want to move too far from the UK. They also wanted somewhere with a lower cost of living than the UK. After extensive research on the internet, they decide to visit Fethiye for a look around. They arranged to see a selection of properties with a local agent. But before starting they made a checklist of what was important for each of them. This was very useful, helping them to decide on the type of property they should be looking for.

"As we were moving permanently we wanted the privacy of our own villa, rather than a complex," says Patricia, who worked as a company secretary in the UK. "Plus, we wanted enough room for friends and family to come and stay." Having a swimming pool was also important to them.

They looked at a number of villas around Fethiye and also made a point of talking to people who had already made the move.

"I'd recommend anyone thinking of buying to take their time and not to commit until they're absolutely sure."

"We found it so useful talking to other English people who had bought in the area," says Patricia. "I would also recommend anyone thinking of buying to take their time and not to commit themselves until they're absolutely sure."

Once they were back in the UK, they decided on one of the properties they had seen - a spacious three-bedroom villa near the beach in Çaliş. On the market for £110,000, the price included all the furniture and appliances. It didn't have a swimming pool, but the garden was large enough to have one put it.

"We decided on Çaliş because it has a year-round community, unlike some of the other resorts," says John.

Having put their houses on the market in Preston, they paid a deposit to the estate agent, only returning once to Fethiye during the entire buying process.

"It all ran like clockwork," remembers Patricia. "And within 4 months we were sitting beside our new swimming pool."

They have both adjusted well to life in Turkey and are enjoying being free of financial concerns. During the winter they started Turkish lessons so they can speak to their new Turkish neighbours.

John and Patricia bought from Taurean Properties, www.taureanproperties.co.uk

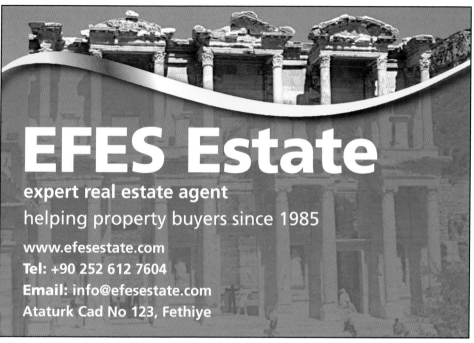

EFES Estate

expert real estate agent

helping property buyers since 1985

www.efesestate.com
Tel: +90 252 612 7604
Email: info@efesestate.com
Ataturk Cad No 123, Fethiye

Kalkan

Overlooking a deep bay, Kalkan has a great location and a good selection of villas at the middle and upper end of the market

KALKAN AT A GLANCE
Population: 3,600
Telephone Area Code: 0242
Airport: Dalaman (2 hours)
Tourist Information: none

PROPERTY LOWDOWN
TYPICAL PRICES:
Apartment (2-bed): £60,000
Villa (3-bed): £150,000
Rental Potential: Fair-Good
Advantages: Scenic location.
Close to excellent beach and tourist attractions. Good rental potential with the right property
Disadvantages: Limited amenities in the off-season. Unsightly development in parts. Poor infrastructure in some areas.

ESTATE AGENTS
Mavi Real Estate:
Tel 0242 8441220
www.kalkanproperty.com

KALKAN IS A SMALL BUT RAPIDLY GROWING resort tumbling down a steep mountainside to a small harbour filled with yachts. The town itself only has a small stretch of pebbly shorefront, though the stunning beach at Patara, and the historical sights of the Xanthos valley, are only a short drive away. Particularly popular with British tourists, many of whom rent villas rather than stay in hotels, Kalkan's narrow streets leading down to the harbour are lined with restaurants, shops and bars. However, many of these close for the winter months, when there are just some basic shops, a small supermarket and medical centre that remain open. On-going improvements to the main coastal highway have cut the journey time to Dalaman airport to around 2 hours.

Kalkan has grown explosively in recent years, with major development on the mountainside above the town centre and along the coast. The housing stock is predominantly villas, with fewer apartments due to local building restrictions. In the old town itself, small stone houses provide atmospheric, if cramped accommodation. A two-bedroom cottage with small courtyard typically sells from £120,000 in this area. Building and renovation work in this area is subject to strict planning controls.

To the west of the town, the quiet residential district of Kalamar Bay has a mix of new and re-sale property, with three-bedroom villas typically available from £110,000-£150,000. There are also some plots available for building.

In the opposite direction, Kışla has excellent views and benefits from cooling sea breezes in summer. However, as with other newly developed areas above the town, access roads and infrastructure are poor at present. Villas above the town benefit from wonderful views and may be within walking distance of the centre. Prices range from £110,000 to over £300,000 depending on the property and location.

In season there is high demand for rental villas in Kalkan, but due to the large number of new properties available a good location, close to town and with a sea view, is crucial for successful rental returns. A four-bedroom villa with pool rents for around £1,000 per week in high-season.

Kalkan's pedestrianised main street winds down to a small harbour

Villas above the town benefit from wonderful views and may be within walking distance of the centre

Enjoying a scenic location, the town has been transformed by rapid development

Expert View
What's so special about Kalkan?

Kalkan is a really friendly resort, with a good community atmosphere. People who visit on holiday tend to return again and again, and now many have bought properties. There is a great choice of restaurants and bars, and the nightlife is more civilised than other resorts. There is lots to do locally too, with some really fascinating sites and unspoilt rural villages within an easy drive of town.

The town centre has some lovely Ottoman and Greek architecture, which is well protected now. Plus almost all the properties have a seaview

Kemal Safyürek is the owner of Mavi Real Estate, www.kalkanproperty.com

due to the town's sloping topography.

Is it still a good investment?
Yes, because the resort maintains its appeal while developing new services and

facilities. Strict zoning also means the land open for development is diminishing quickly, although unlike other resorts, prime plots with great views are still available.

I am expecting at least a 15% increase in prices over the next 12 months.

Where is the best place to buy?
The area of Kışla has excellent potential, with land available and lovely views across the bay to the town. New areas are also being opened up for development in Kalamar Bay.

A Buyer's Tale
Crazy about Kalkan

Bill and Rosemary Erasmus never intended to buy a house in Turkey, but during a break in the relaxed coastal resort of Kalkan in 2001, they decided to look at a few properties.

"We certainly didn't go looking for a villa," remembers Rosemary. "But we'd had lovely holidays in the area, so we thought we'd have a look."

The couple were introduced by a friend to a local teacher who was selling his house. Perched high on the mountainside, with sweeping views over the harbour and glittering Kalamaki Bay, it's easy to see what attracted them to the property.

"We don't normally make hasty decisions, but when we saw that view the place was sold," says Bill

Built as a Turkish family home, the house had two levels divided conveniently into self-contained flats.

It also had planning permission for a third floor, which the Erasmus' added along with a terrace and plunge pool. Inside, the rooms were cramped and dark, so after consulting a local builder Bill and Rosemary decided to remove several internal walls to create a more open feel.

New wood floors, fittings and furniture were the finishing touches to what are now three self-contained apartments, which the couple rent when they're not being used.

Kaputaş is a very popular beach close to Kalkan.

"We don't normally make hasty decisions, but when we saw that view the place was sold"

"It's perfect having the divided space because we can let them individually, or all as one," says Rosemary. "It also means we're not on top of each other when we have guests, or our

grandchildren are here!"

The couple advertise their flats in the local press, with the largest three-bedroom unit fetching £750 a week in high season.

The flats are generally full throughout the summer, when Bill and Rosemary find the weather too hot anyway.

"We spend about 8 weeks a year here now," says Rosemary. "Though it's generally in October and March,".

As well as fantastic views from their villa, Bill and Rosemary love the friendly, laid-back atmosphere of Kalkan, with the prospect of meeting old friends drawing them back each year.

MAVI
REAL ESTATE AND MORE...

www.kalkanproperty.com

MAVI is a professional Turkish-British estate agency with the most comprehesive portfolio in Kalkan and its neighbouring towns and villages ranging from affordable apartments as low as £ 27,500 to luxury villas. Please visit our web site for all details or pop in our offices in Kalkan for a friendly chat.
Email :info@kalkanproperty.com Telefax :0090 242 8442456 Mob: 0532 26122 96

This truly exceptional property, located adjacent to and with direct access to the sea, has exquistely landscaped gardens and sweeping panaromic views from every levels. Please visit www.kalkanproperty.com

Kaş

A small seaside town on an unspoilt stretch of coast, Kaş has a good choice of villas, apartments and land

KAŞ AT A GLANCE
Population: 8,000
Telephone Area Code: 0242
Airport: Dalaman (2.5 hours)
Tourist Information: none

PROPERTY LOWDOWN
TYPICAL PRICES:
Apartment (2-bed): £65,000
Villa (3-bed): £175,000
Rental Potential: Fair-Good
Advantages: Picturesque coastal town. Unspoilt rural hinterland Good year-round amenities
Disadvantages:
Far from the airport
No good beaches.
Poor medical facilities.

ESTATE AGENTS
Sun Estate Agent
Tel 0242 8361597,
www.sunestate-tr.com

KasLand
Tel 0242 8363779,
www.kasland.com

BACKED BY ROCKY MOUNTAINS, Kaş is a relaxed seaside town overlooking the Greek island of Meis. Formely a fishing and market centre, tourism now dominates the local economy. Despite this, it hasn't been swamped by mass tourism and retains much of its original character and charm. Sitting on the site of ancient Antiphellus, the town is dotted with archaeological remains, including a small amphitheatre and monumental tombs. The local coastline is rocky and beaches are limited to short pebble stretches. The nearby countryside is scattered with interesting archaeological sites and Kaş is an excellent base for adventure activities.

Kaş has a well-established expatriate community, which is swelled in summer by European and Turkish tourists. There is a good selection of restaurants and shops, with several small supermarkets and a colourful weekly market for fresh produce. Medical facilities are limited to a small health centre, with the nearest hospital in Fethiye, a 90-minute drive away.

Reaching out towards Greek Meis, the 7 km Çukurbağ Peninsular is one of the most desirable areas to buy in Kaş. Originally owned by the Turkish Association of Journalists, development on the peninsular has been strictly controlled, with limits on the height and extent of building. Remaining undeveloped plots (approximately 1,500 m2) are very rare and sell for over £110,000. Enjoying a quiet location and lovely sea views, villas on the peninsular typically fetch from £160,000-£250,000 for three-bedrooms, sometimes considerably more. Without a car, access into town is limited to an hourly minibus service which runs summer-only.

The centre of town has a mix of re-sale and new-build apartments and villas, with prices significantly lower than on the peninsular. These properties have the advantage of easy access to all the town's

facilities, although noise can be a problem during the summer months in some areas.

Above the main town, Çerçiler is an area of newly built apartments and villas. These benefit from excellent views and prices are lower than elsewhere. However, care should be taken to check that properties have proper title deeds and planning consent, as many have been constructed illegally on state land. Gökseki, to the west of Kaş, has only recently been surveyed and title deeds have yet to be issued. Rental potential is best on the Çukurbağ Peninsular due to its quiet location and stunning views. Year-round lets are also possible in the town centre.

Kemer

A purpose built resort set in some of the Turquoise Coast's most stunning scenery, with good beaches and forested mountains

Kemer's town centre and marina area are carefully planned, but lack atmosphere

KEMER AT A GLANCE
Population: 17,000
Telephone Area Code: 0242
Airport: Antalya (1 hour)
Tourist Information:
Belediye Binası
Tel 0242 8141537

PROPERTY LOWDOWN
TYPICAL PRICES:
Apartment (2-bed): £60,000
Villa (3-bed): £125,000
Rental Potential: Fair
Advantages:
Beautiful surroundings.
Close to Antalya airport
Disadvantages:
The town lacks atmosphere.
Limited rental market

ESTATE AGENTS
JFC Properties:
Tel (UK) 0161 343 7700
www.jfcproperties.co.uk

LOCATED 35 km SOUTHWEST of Antalya, Kemer is a state-planned resort of hotels and apartment complexes. Built since the 1980s, the town center is well laid-out but lacks atmosphere. It boasts good facilities, including a modern marina, lots of shops and several beaches, with a Blue Flag awarded stretch in the town itself. The town's mountainous hinterland, much of it preserved within the Beydağ ları National Park, is exceptionally beautiful and has some excellent walking. The Lycian Way long distance footpath passes close to the town. Nearby sights include the remains of Phaselis, an important ancient city visited by Alexander the Great.

Kemer is particularly popular with Russian tourists, although most of the area's property buyers come from Germany. British buyers are concentrated in the smaller resort of Çamyuva, 5 km south of the town center. Kemer has a supermarket and private medical facilities. Regular public minibuses link the resort to Antalya, which is under an hour away by car.

Properties in the center of town are mostly resale apartments with renovated units available from £40,000-£70,000, or from £70,000 on the seafront. New apartments and off-plan developments can be found in the area of Aslanbuçak, 2 km inland from the centre. Prices are significantly lower there, with a two-bedroom apartment typically selling for £30,000, although local agents report that rental potential is much better in the center. The rental market is mostly short-term holiday lets and a managing agent with marketing connections in Russia would be necessary for good returns.

Due to local planning restrictions in Çamyuva, small apartment compexes and large detached villas are the most common property types. The apartments generally have communal facilities, such as swimming pools. Prices for a large three-bedroom house with pool generally range from £100,000-£130,000, with larger properties available from £140,000. Apartments typically start from £35,000 for two bedrooms. Land with building permission is also available in the Çamyuva area.

East Mediterranean & Cappadocia

Antalya&Belek

Shopping, beaches, nightlife and an atmospheric old quarter - the city of Antalya has it all, as well as golf courses at nearby Belek

ANTALYA AT A GLANCE
Population: 603,000
Telephone Area Code: 0242
Airport: Antalya (15 mins)
Tourist Information:
Cumhuriyet Caddesi,
Özel Idare Altı No 2,
Tel 0242 2475042

PROPERTY LOWDOWN
TYPICAL PRICES:
Apartment (2-bed): £65,000
Villa (3-bed): £130,000
Rental Potential: Fair-Good
Advantages: Excellent facilities
and shopping. Year-round city.
Large choice of property
Disadvantages:
Large, congested urban center
Expensive in some areas

ESTATE AGENTS
Turkish Homes:
Tel (UK) 0845 331 2644
www.turkish-homes.com

A RAPIDLY GROWING CITY of over 1/2 million people, Antalya is the main administrative and commercial center for most of the Mediterranean coast. The city's modern airport is an important gateway, receiving hundreds of thousands of arrivals from across Europe each year. Sprawling around a wide bay, with the Taurus mountains as a backdrop, the city enjoys a dramatic setting.

Kaleiçi, which literally means "Inside the Castle", is the historic heart of the city. Surrounded by the old city walls, its narrow streets are lined with Ottoman timber-frame houses, many of which have been renovated or converted into hotels. The old harbour has also been tastefully redeveloped and is surrounded by cafes, shops and restaurants. The buildings of this area enjoy official protection, so any renovation or building work is tightly controlled.

West of the center, Konyaaltı has a long pebble beach lined with cafes, bars and entertainment venues, with a large water-park nearby. The city's other main beach is 12 km east of the center at Lara. The city has several large, modern shopping centres.

Antalya's property market is dominated by modern apartments. Prices vary hugely according to the location. A two-bedroom apartment costs from £35,000 in an inland location, rising to over £110,000 in a luxury block on the sea front in Lara. Lara and Konyaaltı are the most desirable areas, and some apartment blocks have swimming pools and other facilities. For those in search of an Ottoman house to restore, Kaleiçi and the area of Haşim Işcan, just outside the city walls, are the places to look. Prices depend on the size and condition of the building, but it is difficult to find a real bargain these days.

Belek, 30 km east of Antalya, has become Turkey's foremost golfing area, with six international standard courses now in operation. Designated as a tourism development area by the government, a string of large resort hotels dominate the coast, blocking access to the excellent sandy beaches in some places. Behind the wooded coastal strip villa developments have sprung-up on agricultural land. Golf aside, facilities and shopping are very poor in the immediate area at present.

There are a number of new and off-plan developments with excellent facilities in the area. Prices range from £75,000 to over £100,000 for a three-bedroom complex villa, or from £40,000 for a two-bedroom apartment bought off-plan. Older resale villas are available from £50,000, but the quality of build is generally low and they may not make a good long-term investment. With its status as a golfing center and improving local facilities, rental potential may develop in the future, although at present it is poor due to competition from the many resort hotels in the area.

A Buyer's Tale
A Labour of Love

Kate Clow, a British writer and guide based in Antalya, was renting a modern apartment when a friend suggested buying an old house in the historic Haşım Işcan district of the city. "I went to see the house and liked it, although it was in a very bad state," says Kate.

Little did she know that it would be two years before she owned the house, and another year before she actually moved in. Like many old properties in Turkey, the house had been inherited by a large number of people from the same family – fourteen to be exact. Over the years, the old woman living in the house had lost touch with her relatives, however, the law required all of their consent before the sale could proceed. As the principal owner, the woman applied to the courts and after a lengthy investigation the house was cleared for sale in a government auction.

"It was a nerve racking experience," remembers Kate, who luckily speaks excellent Turkish. "As I was bidding against two other people." But she made the winning bid and bought the 80 year-old house for €23,000 (£15,000). Located in an old neighbourhood just outside the city walls, her new acquisition was in need of urgent attention. Subsidence had caused the back of the house to sink, and rain was pouring in through the

"We had to rebuild the entire house... new plumbing, wiring and windows, two main walls, and, of course, the roof."

roof. Kate decided to divide the house into two apartments, so she could rent out one and live in the other. She wanted to retain as many of the original features, such as the beautiful wooden ceilings, as possible, though most of the interior would have to go. She employed an architect to draw up the plans and apply for permission to carry out the necessary work. Situated in a special conservation area, the proposals had to be passed by a committee from the Ministry of Culture's Environmental Preservation Institute, as well as the local planning authority. This took over 3 months, but work finally began in earnest in December 2001, and lasted until June of the following year: "We basically had to rebuild the entire house," says Kate. "Adding new plumbing, wiring and windows, as well as two of the main external walls, and, of course, the roof."

In total the work cost €25,000 (£17,000), but she now has two atmospheric apartments, one of which she rents out.

"I love the fact that the house is so central, within 5 minutes walk of the sea, the old town and the city centre, yet it's very peaceful and has a garden."

Kate Clow is the inspiration behind Turkey's first long distance footpaths, the Lycian Way and St Paul Trail. For more information visit www.trekkinginturkey.com

Side

Once an important Roman city, Side is now a family beach resort with a good selection of apartments and villas around it

SIDE AT A GLANCE
Population: 16,400
Telephone Area Code: 0242
Airport: Antalya (45 mins)
Tourist Information:
Side Yolu Uzeri
Tel 0242 7531265

PROPERTY LOWDOWN
TYPICAL PRICES:
Apartment (2-bed): £55,000
Villa (3-bed): £85,000
Rental Potential: Fair
Advantages:
Easy airport access.
Good beaches and activities.
A wide choice of apartments.
Disadvantages:
Quiet in the off-season.
Some properties are a long way
from the resort.

ESTATE AGENTS
Properties in Turkey:
Tel 0242 7536517
www.propertiesinturkey.com

SITTING ON A SMALL PENINSULAR, 65 km east of Antalya, Side is a popular family beach resort that has grown up beside the atmospheric remains of an ancient Roman city. The main street, lined with touristy shops and boutiques, descends to a small harbour overlooked by restaurants and bars. The ruins of ancient Side, including an impressive amphitheatre and the Temple of Apollo, are scattered around the centre and there is a well-stocked local archaeological museum. Sandy beaches stretch along the coast in either direction, attracting thousands of European and Turkish holidaymakers each summer. In addition to excellent water sports, leisure activities in the area include horse riding and white water rafting. The golf courses of Belek are a 25-minute drive away, with a new course planned for the Side area itself.

Many of the shops and restaurants in Side are closed during the winter and the area is very quiet off-season. There are supermarkets open year-round on the main highway and in the nearby town of Manavgat, which also has a large weekly market.

Due to the scarcity of land and the historic ruins around the center, development has spread along the coast to the east and west of the resort, as well as inland towards the coastal highway. Local planning regulations restrict building to between two and four storeys depending on the area. Much of the most recent development has been apartment complexes, which often have excellent on-site facilities. Some villas are also available on complexes and the area also has some large well-established cooperative developments, built primarily for the Turkish market in the last 15 years.

Prices have risen dramatically in the area with increases of up to 50% in the last 2 years. Two-bedroom apartments are particularly popular and fetch £45,000-£60,000, with three-bedroom apartments on a fully serviced complex typically from £70,000. Seaside apartments are significantly more expensive. There are comparatively few villas being built with prices generally starting from £85,000, although a luxury detached house with pool can sell for upwards of £110,000. Despite often requiring some renovation work, properties on the older cooperative developments can represent excellent value with a three-bedroom semi-detached house from £45,000. The local rental season is June to September, with weekly rates of £250 for a two-bedroom apartment, and £350 for a three-bedroom apartment.

The Temple of Apollo is one of the area's historic attractions

A Buyer's Tale
Cooperative Heaven

When Michael and Barbara Harrison decided to buy a property abroad they cast their minds back to a happy beach holiday spent in Side. "We had a great time, with the lovely beaches and friendly people," remembers Barbara. "So we decided this would be the perfect place to start looking." Although their main aim was to have a holiday home to enjoy with their daughter and son-in-law, they also wanted a good investment. After researching on the internet, they contacted a local agent and arranged to view some properties. One of the first was on a large, well-established villa development, 10 km east of Side. Built in 1995 as part of a cooperative for Turkish families, the three-bedroom, two-bathroom semi-detached house was exactly what the couple were looking for: "We liked the Turkish style of the house with all the living space on the upper floor," says Michael. "It's cooler in summer as the terrace catches any breeze." Although the house needed modernization, it was well below their budget of £30,000. As part of a well-established cooperative development, it had an individual title deed, with services such as 24-hour security and a large communal pool funded by a £45 monthly service fee. Michael insisted on having the property surveyed by a local architect and builder – an unusual request in Turkey – however, the house past this inspection and the sale was

The Harrisons bought from Properties in Turkey, www.propertiesinturkey.com

"We liked the Turkish style of the house with all the living space on the upper floor"

completed. "The most important thing for us was having a good agent, and an English-speaking solicitor," says Michael. "They did most of the running around, and everything went smoothly."

Soon after taking possession, Michael and Barbara had a builder replace the bathroom and kitchen units and lay new tiles throughout the house. They also enclosed the external staircase, added a third bathroom and seating area to the top-floor, installed air-conditioning and had a pergola built on the terrace. The cost of the work was very reasonable," says Michael. "We spent about £15,000 in all." The Harrisons now spend 3 months in Side each year. One of twenty other British families on the development, they enjoy socializing with their neighbours, sightseeing and Michael is a keen diver.

Alanya

A view of Alanya's harbour district from the town's medieval castle walls

With its excellent beaches and facilities, investors and private buyers have been flooding into Alanya's property market

ALANYA IS ONE OF THE LARGEST RESORTS on the Turkish Mediterranean coast. Formerly the winter capital of the Selçuk Turkish empire, the modern town has grown rapidly in the shadow of a large medieval castle built on a sea-girt rock which dominates the coast for miles in each direction. In addition to the historic interest of the castle and city walls, Alanya has excellent leisure facilities and good beaches, including several Blue Flag-awarded stretches. The town's lively nightlife is centered on the harbour area, where there is a wide choice of restaurants, bars and clubs. There are also lots of shops and a large weekly market.

Alanya has grown rapidly in the last 15 years with development now stretching for more than 20 km along the coast. Particularly popular with Scandinavian, Dutch and German package tourists and property buyers, the town now has over 9,000 foreign residents, with an increasing number of Irish and British entering the market. Attracted by the warm climate, many retirees now spend the winter months in the resort, with families and younger buyers attracted by the beaches and entertainment in summer.

The property stock is mainly apartments, with lots of new-builds

ALANYA AT A GLANCE
Population: 88,000
Telephone Area Code: 0242
Airport: Antalya (1.5 hours)
Tourist Information:
Damlataş Caddesi No 1
Tel 0242 5131240

PROPERTY LOWDOWN

TYPICAL PRICES:

Apartment (2-bed): £50,000

Villa (3-bed): £85,000

Rental Potential: Good

Advantages: Good beaches and activities. Year-round facilities. Good choice of property, particularly apartments.

Disadvantages: Urban setting. Poor infrastructure in some areas. Relatively few villas.

ESTATE AGENTS

Let's Go To Turkey:

Tel 0242 5132064

www.letsgototurkey.com

M&C Property:

Tel 0532 2062928

www.mandcproperty.com

Tolerance Realty:

Tel 0242 5193056

www.tolerancerealty.com

and off-plan developments. In the center, most of the properties are resale apartments, often over 7 years old and in need of renovation. Prices start from £35,000 for a resale three-bedroom apartment, though expect to pay over £50,000 for a similar property near the beach. An additional £10,000-£15,000 could secure you a sea view. You will also pay a premium for apartments on the lower slopes of the castle rock, which benefit from views and greener surroundings.

To the east of the center, the suburb of Oba has a good beach and shopping and easy access to the center. Nearby Cikcili has recently been opened-up for development. Bought off-plan, two-bedroom apartments on well-equipped complexes typically start from £50,000 in these areas.

Mahmutlar, 15 km east of the center, is a small but rapidly growing resort. Apartment blocks and villa complexes have sprouted in the last 5 years from the banana plantations inland of the main highway. Prices are 15-20% lower than in Alanya, although the basic infrastructure is lacking in many areas. Due to the huge amount of new property, older resale apartments should be avoided by investment buyers. A new two-bedroom, two-bathroom apartment on a complex with shared pool starts from £40,000, or from £65,000 in a sea front location.

Thanks to a long holiday season and a growing influx of winter residents from Scandinavia, the local rental market is buoyant. Three-bedroom furnished apartments typically rent for £200-£400 per week depending on the location and facilities.

Expert View
What's so special about Alanya?

Alanya is a large coastal town which has developed into a major tourist resort, so we have excellent services and facilities open year-round, unlike other smaller Turkish resorts.

There is a good mix of property, from city-centre apartments, to new-build villas and apartment complexes in suburban areas. Property prices are extremely competitive compared to other parts of Turkey.

A large number of Europeans live in the town, and they are now an important part of the community, with increasing involvement in civic affairs.

Taylan Gundeşlioğlu is owner of Let's Go To Turkey, www.letsgototurkey.com

Is it a good investment?

Alanya has seen consistent price rises over the last few years due to major interest from investors and private buyers. This is unlikely to change as new land

available for development near the centre is becoming increasingly hard to find.

A solid rental income can also be generated, with short-term holiday lets or longer rentals to people living and working in the town.

What are the best areas to buy?

There are some very exciting off-plan developments in Oba, Cikcilli and Mahmutlar, which offer excellent potential for capital growth, as these are emerging areas. Town-centre property is a very safe investment due to high demand.

Riveside Resort

from 83k€ £55k

from 120k€ £80k

from 55k€ £37k

Villa Marmaris

Live your dream in Turkey! Little Venice

New investors and agents are always welcome! If you would like to receive further information, please contact us direct!

m&c
Professional Property Service

M&C Professional Property Service
Hacikadiroglu cd.
Asta Residence apt. No:9/43
Alanya/Antalya/Turkey
Tel: 0090 532 206 29 28
colin@mandcproperty.com
www.mandcproperty.com

A Buyer's Tale
Alanya Off-plan

Karl Mahmood had never been to Turkey, but he wanted to buy an investment property in the Mediterranean. After doing some initial research he decided that Alanya, with its beaches and varied leisure activities was the right place to start looking.

"I flew out for 10 days to have an initial look in sprIng 2004," says Karl. "I knew exactly what I wanted and set myself a strict budget."

He viewed dozens of properties with several different estate agents, but found that what he wanted, a villa with it's own pool and a good view, was just beyond his budget.

"I realized that I was going to have to sacrifice something, so I decided to look at some villas on a complex."

"I realized that I was going to have to sacrifice something, so I decided to look at some villas on a complex."

Although these didn't have private swimming pools, Karl was immediately impressed by the facilities available and in the quality of the construction. At €83,000 (£55,000) the properties were also within his budget.

"There were several off-plan villas which were part of the final phase of the development, so I decided on the position I liked best."

Returning to the UK, Karl discussed things with his partner Julia and had the contract, drawn up by the estate agent before his departure, looked over by solicitors. The law firm also ran background checks on the property company, before he decided to sign the contract and transfer a 10% deposit to the company's bank account.

"You are dealing with people that you don't know in another country," says Karl. "You have to be completely confident that everything is secure."

Once the deposit was paid, Karl couldn't believe how quickly things progressed. Within 8 weeks the military checks had been approved. He flew back out in August to visit the registry office with the estate agent and collect his title deeds. By now the villa was starting to take shape and over the following months the estate agent would email regularly with photographs of the building progress.

The villa was completed in October 2004, when Karl, Julia and their 18-month old son, Essam, went out to Alanya to take possession and pay the final instalment. The estate agent took them to a local furniture outlet, where they kitted out the entire property: "We were amazed that everything was delivered the next day!"

The three-bedroom villa is spread out over three floors and has lots of space for family and friends. The complex has a large pool and security. They are renting the villa out during the summer season.

Karl and Julia bought from M&C Property, www.mandcproperty.com

Cappadocia

Cave houses for renovation in a magical landscape with a fascinating history stretching back thousands of years

CAPPADOCIA IS ONE OF the country's most unusual places to buy property. Located in Central Turkey, south east of Ankara, the region has an amazing landscape of eroded valleys, canyons and pinnacles carved from the soft volcanic rock. Protected within a National Park, the area has a rich history dating back thousands of years and is dotted with ancient underground cities and subterranean churches. At an altitude of over 1,000m, the climate is cold and snowy in the winter, with cooler summers than on the coast.

Until recent times many of the local people still lived partially below ground in houses cut from the rock. Most of these cave houses have now been abandoned or have been turned into hotels catering for the thousands of tourists who flock to the area each year. A small but growing number of the traditional Cappadocian houses are also being transformed into atmospheric homes. The main focus of this activity is around the villages of Göreme and Uçhisar, which are surrounded by the area's most beautiful terrain. Formerly small farming communities, traditional rural life continues beside the tourist shops, restaurants and guesthouses. Cave houses in these areas are highly sought after and prices have rocketed in the last 5 years. Nearby villages, such as Çavuşin and Ortahisar, still have cave houses at prices starting from £20,000. However, the cheaper properties may be in an advanced state of dereliction and require almost complete re-building. Building regulations are extremely tight due to the area's historic and geological importance and any plans will be carefully vetted. The best renovations retain the charming original features of the houses, while incorporating modern facilities, such as central heating and en-suite bathrooms.

Most of the old properties in Cappadocia belong to local families and prices can vary wildly depending on location, state of repair, but also the financial position of the owner. Properties are generally sold by word-of-mouth and keen bargaining skills are required to get a fair price. Potential buyers should spend plenty of time exploring the area and enlist the help of a trustworthy local person.

The towns of Ürgüp and Avanos have old stone houses, many of which also require extensive renovation. They are less picturesque communities, but have more shops and services than the villages mentioned above. The provincial town of Nevşehir and the city of Kayseri have extensive shopping, as well as airports served by domestic flights from Istanbul and Ankara.

CAPPADOCIA AT A GLANCE
Population: 350,000
Telephone Area Code: 0384
Airport: Nevşehir /Kayseri (30 / 90 mins)
Tourist Information:
Atatürk Bulvarı, Nevşehir
Tel 0384 2139604

PROPERTY LOWDOWN
TYPICAL PRICES:
Apartment (2-bed): N/A
Villa (3-bed): N/A
Rental Potential: Poor

ESTATE AGENTS:
Avatar International:
Tel: 08707 282827,
www.avatar-international.com

Hot air ballooning is one way of exploring the magical landscape

A Buyer's Tale
Cave Living

Hot air balloon pilots, Kaili Kidner and Lars-Eric Möre fly thousands of tourists over the magical landscape of Cappadocia at dawn every year. The couple had been working in the area for six years before they even thought of buying a home there. Working a gruelling schedule, they'd been living in an apartment above their office in the village of Göreme. But all that changed in 1997, when Lars went to the local shop: "He went out to buy some bread and came back with a house," laughs Kaili.

A chance meeting in the shop led to Lars and Kaili buying a small cave house burrowed from one of the area's 'fairy chimneys', an eroded pinnacles of rock, for £2,000 – a fraction of what it would cost today. "It was more of a ruin than a house," admits Kaili. "But we immediately saw the potential."

Situated in the upper part of the village, where the cave dwellings and eroded rock formations are strictly protected, the rooms were filled with rubbish and there was no roof on the external part of the structure. Even more worrying were the signs of cracking in the fairy chimney itself.

"Once we'd removed the rubbish, we had to apply for permission to make the

A chance meeting in the shop led to them buying a small cave house burrowed from a 'fairy chimney'

necessary changes," says Lars. The couple wanted to create a comfortable home, while making as few changes to the physical fabric of the structure as possible. A supporting wall helped stabilise the fairy chimney and a new roof and several new windows were added. They employed a local foreman to organise the craftsmen and stonemasons, while their Turkish employees helped keep an eye on progress.

"It is really important to be on-site as much as possible," says Kaili. "If you're not around then costs have a tendency to spiral."

They managed to buy the property next-door, allowing them to expand the house into a spacious two-bedroom home with a large livingroom, kitchen and dining area. Many of the rooms are built into the rock and others have stone arched ceilings. The house is centrally heated, an important feature during the bitterly cold Cappadocian winters.

They finally moved into their new home in 2003, having spent about £50,000 on the transformation.

"The house has a peaceful atmosphere," says Kaili. "Though during the summer we're so busy that we have very little time to appreciate it."

For information about ballooning visit: www.kapadokyaballoons.com

Istanbul & Information

Istanbul

A metropolis with a foot on two continents, Istanbul has a huge choice of property from old apartments to modern luxury homes

ISTANBUL AT A GLANCE
Population: 12,000,000
Telephone Area Code:
0212 (Europe) 0216 (Asia)
Airport: Atatürk Havalımanı
(20-60 mins)
Tourist Information
Atatürk Airport
Tel: 0212 6630793
Beyoğlu
Meşrutiyet Caddesi 57, Floor 7
Tel: 0212 2433472

PROPERTY LOWDOWN
TYPICAL PRICES:
Apartment (2-bed): $250,000
Villa (3-bed): $450,000
Rental Potential: Good
Advantages: Cosmopolitan city.
Large choice of property.
Excellent rental potential
in many areas.
Disadvantages: Large, congested
urban center. High prices.

ESTATE AGENTS
Istanbul Accommodation
Centre:
Tel 0212 2928944
www.istanbul
accommodationcentre.com
Mavi Ay Real Estate:
Tel 0212 3252056
www.maviayestate.com
Remax
Tel 0212 2324820
www.remax.com.tr/en

SPANNING TWO CONTINENTS and divided by the waters of the Bosphorus and the Golden Horn, Istanbul is the undisputed commercial, industrial and cultural heart of Turkey. With a history dating back over 5,000 years, the city was the capital of the Byzantine and Ottoman empires and has a rich legacy of castles, palaces and mosques, plus several world-class museum collections, which attract millions of tourists each year. Its present-day population is 12 million - and growing fast. A staggering 700,000 migrants arrive in the city each year. Flying in to the city's Atatürk airport on a clear day you can see the urban sprawl for miles along the Sea of Marmara coast.

In a city growing so quickly there is immense demand for housing and prices are higher than anywhere else in the country. The introduction of a mortgage system is expected to encourage demand still further. As the regional base for many multinational corporations, the city has a large expatriate community, who often live in suburban villas or the pleasant Bosphorus villages. The city's growing middle-class also favour suburban developments, though these are usually apartments with schools, shopping and entertainment nearby. In the inner city neighbourhoods, neglected 19th century apartment buildings are being renovated by young professionals and foreigners.

As you would expect in a city this size, Istanbul has a huge choice of property. Within walking distance of city centre nightlife and entertainment, the apartment buildings of Cihangir are popular with foreign buyers. In nearby Beyoğlu, a wealthy European suburb during Ottoman times, the narrow roads leading off Istiklal Caddesi, the city's main shopping street, are lined with graceful, but neglected buildings. Poor and seedy, Istanbul's answer to Soho is enjoying a revival, with café culture and nightlife in full swing. Many apartments have become the target for renovation, though the process can be fraught with difficulties in such a densely populated area. Further south, Galata has more old apartments, many with great potential for renovators.

The prize in all these areas is a Bosphorus view from a roof terrace or balcony, for which you pay a hefty premium. Prices, which are generally in local currency or US dollars, range from about $1,000 (£550) per m2 to at least double that for an apartment with a view. Unconverted properties currently sell for about $500-$1,000 (£550-£1,100) per m2.

In contrast to the inner city neighbourhoods, the Bosphorus suburbs have more space and a more relaxed pace of life. Formerly villages and home to the Ottoman gentry in summer, the pleasant waterside location of Bebek, Kanlıca and Yeniköy brings with it a large price tag. These areas are home to some of the city's wealthiest residents. They are also home to some of the city's most beautiful Ottoman residences, the wooden *yalı*, which typically stand right on the water's edge.

Inland on the European shore, Etiler and Levent are desirable suburbs with good shopping facilities and easy access to the city's main business district. Levent also has the advantage of being on the metro line allowing easy access into Taksim square and the center of town.

Prices in all these desirable neighbourhoods start from $1,500 (£825) per m2, though nice apartments and houses typically start from $3,000 (£1,650) per m2, and often much, much more.

Further out, areas such as Zekeriyaköy and Kemerburgaz have low density suburban housing, which is popular with wealthy Turkish families and expatriates. There are usually good schools and sports facilities in the vicinity, but a car is essential.

Prices typically start from $2,500-$3,000 (£1,350-£1,650) per m2 in these wealthy suburbs, with the most desirable homes selling for in excess of $1,000,000 (£550,000).

Prime real estate - the Topkapı Palace, home of the Ottoman sultans

Newly-built apartment complexes in areas like Ataşehir and Bahçeşehir are in huge demand by middle-class Turkish buyers. Prices typically range from $1,500-$2,500 (£825-£1,350) per m2, and the developments generally have good facilities.

Istanbul's rental market is extremely buoyant. Rates vary hugely depending on location and, in areas near the Bosphorus, whether the property has a view. In Cihangir and Beyoğlu, for example, there is strong demand from foreigners with monthly rates from $700-$2,000 (£380-£1,000). In the Bosphorus suburbs prices range from $1,000- over $5,000 (£550-£2,750) per month. The classified section of the Turkish Daily News is a good place to look for rental agents and properties.

The prize in these areas is a Bosphorus view from a roof terrace or balcony, for which you pay a hefty premium

A Buyer's Tale
An Istanbul Eyrie

As a journalist based in Istanbul but travelling constantly, Rupert Birch decided in 2001 that he wanted to buy an apartment in the city. "I needed somewhere to get away from it all when I had time off," explains Rupert. He began looking in Galata, just north of the Golden Horn. Historically the city's commercial and banking district, the area fell on hard times, with its narrow streets becoming rundown and seedy. But within walking distance of Istanbul's main shopping street and nightlife, Galata has become popular in the last decade with young Turkish and foreign buyers. Restaurants and bars have opened locally, and a lively café culture has developed.
"I wanted something cheap that I could renovate in a central location," says Rupert. "Galata ticked all the boxes."
After several weeks looking he found a top-floor apartment near the historic Genoese watchtower. It was in a terrible state of repair: "It had no electricity, the roof was leaking and the floor boards were rotten," remembers Rupert. "But we got it for a very low price, allowing me more to spend on the renovation."
Rupert was recommended a solicitor to handled the conveyancing, and within 2 months the apartment was his for $13,000. Some friends suggested an architect who had converted other apartments locally, and she

Rupert enjoying the view of Istanbul's old city from his roof terrace

"I wanted to find something cheap which I could renovate in a centrally located area"

drew-up plans for a two-bedroom apartment, with a roof-terrace to take advantage of the sweeping views. This involved gutting the interior, raising the roof and replacing the steel beams

supporting the floor, which had corroded. As work progressed it became obvious that the builder had underestimated the costs in his quote. This is not unusual in complex renovation projects and Rupert agreed to pay for some unforeseen expenses, which took the total bill to $30,000. The work also took longer than expected, though the apartment was eventually ready a year after he'd bought it.
Rupert remains happy with the results, while rising property prices in Galata have made it a sound investment too. Although he spends less than 3 months in the apartment each year, it is a place he can call home.

Directorywww.buyinginturkey.info

VISIT OUR ONLINE DIRECTORY

AIRLINES & TRAVEL
Alternative Travel
Tel 08700 411448
www.alternativeturkey.com
British Airways
Tel 0870 8509850
www.ba.com
Turkish Airlines
Tel 020 77669300
www.thy.com.tr
Turkish Cyprus Airlines
Tel 020 7930 4851
www.kthy.net

AIRLINES (Charter)
Avro
Tel 0870 4582841
www.avro.co.uk
Excel
Tel 0870 1690169
www.xl.com
Monarch
Tel 08700 405040
www.flymonarch.com
MyTravel
Tel 0870 238 7777
www.mytravel.com
Thomas Cook
Tel 08707505711
www.thomascook.com

AIRLINES (Domestic)
Atlas Jet
Tel 0216 4440387
www.atlasjet.com/eng
Flyair
Tel 0212 4444359
www.flyair.com.tr
Onur Air
Tel 0212 6629797
www.onurair.com.tr

BANKS
Citibank
Tel 444 0500
www.citibank.com.tr

Finans Bank
Tel 444 0900
www.finansbank.com.tr
Garanti Bank
Tel 444 0333
www.garantibank.com
Yapı ve Kredi
Tel 4440444
www.yapikredi.com/en

BUS COMPANIES
Ulusoy
Tel 444 8999
www.ulusoy.com.tr/eng/
Varan
Tel 444 1888
www.varan.com.tr

CAR RENTAL
Avis
Tel 0212 3686800
www.avis.com.tr
Bougainville Turizm
Tel 0242 836 3737
www.bougainville-turkey.com
Real Tours/Europcar
Tel 0252 6144995
www.realtour.com.tr
Sixt
Tel 0212 3189040
www.sunrent.com

COURIER COMPANIES
Aras
Tel 0216 5385555
www.araskargo.com/en/
TNT
Tel 0216 4251700
www.tnt.com
UPS
Tel 0212 4440033
www.ups.com.tr

DEVELOPERS & CONSTRUCTION
Ada İnşaat
Tel 0252 3161180
ada.mimarlik@turk.net

Çağdaş Group
Tel 0252 3135470
www.cagdasgroup.com
Çakmak Construction
Tel 01954 202103 (UK)
www.turkey-estate.com
Costello Construction
Tel 0242 5143565
www.costelloconstructiontr.com
Curbanoğlu
Tel 0871 7113919 (UK local rate)
www.curbanoglu.com
Dolphin Homes
Tel 0256 8131697
www.dolphinhomesinturkey.com
Hanel Houses
Tel 0252 6148810
www.hanelhouses.com
Mecitoğlu Homes
Tel 0242 7533910
www.homeinturkey.com
Öz Cebeci
Tel 0533 4944401
www.alanyacebeci.com
Pera Mimarlık
Tel 0212 2516430
www.peramim.com
Tandem İnşaat
Tel 0242 8363287
www.tandemvillas.com

ESTATE AGENTS
UK & General
Aquavista
Tel 01580 850170
www.aquavistaproperty.com
Avatar International
Tel 08707 282827
www.avatar-turkey.com
Headlands International
Tel 0845 9005151
www.headlands.co.uk
Try Turkey
Tel 01384 341444
www.tryturkey.co.uk
Turkish Connextions
Tel: 01772 735151
www.turkishconnextions.co.uk

Turkish Homes UK
Tel 0845 331 2644
www.turkish-homes.com
Turyap
www.turyap.com.tr/english/

ESTATE AGENTS
**Aegean: Ayvalık, Çeşme,
Altınkum,Kuşadası, Bodrum**
Ayvalık Property
Tel: 01622-764200,
www.ayvalikproperty.com
Başkent Estate
Tel 256 6147311
www.baskentemlak.com
Cumberland Properties
Tel 0207 4358113 (UK local rate)
www.cumberland-properties.com
Expert Real Estate
Tel 0256 6131770
www.turkeyexpert.co.uk
Kuşadası Property Sales
Tel 0256 612 3263
www.kusadasipropertysales.com
Golden Sun Homes
Tel 0256 8136558
www.goldensunhomes.com
Ibak Homes
Tel 0252 3822294
www.ibakhomes.com
Mavi Emlak
Tel 0252 3134098
www.maviemlak.net
My Turkish Home
Tel 0256 8132330
www.myturkishhome.com
Turkish Homes
Tel 0256 8133460
www.turkish-homes.com
Turkish Property Centre
Tel 0256 813 1210
www.turkishpropertycentre.com
Turyap
www.turyap.com.tr/english/
Villas in Turkey
Tel 0232 7122326
www.villasinturkey.net

ESTATE AGENTS
**West Mediterranean: Marmaris,
Dalaman, Fethiye, Kalkan, Kaş**
Cartier Real Estate
Tel 0252 4552979
www.icmelerestateagency.com
Dalaman Estates
Tel 0252 6923561
www.dalamanestates.co.uk
Efes Estate
Tel 0252 6127604
www.efesestate.com
Falcon Estates
Tel 0252 616 6436
www.falconestates.net
Hanel Houses
Tel 0252 6148810
www.hanelhouse.com
Lagoon Estates
Tel 0252 6129193
www.lagoonestates.com
Mavi Real Estate
Tel 0242 8441220
www.kalkanproperty.com
Nicholas Homes
Tel 0252 6167455
www.nicholas-homes.com
Red-Tek Real Estate
Tel 0252 4130422
www.redtekrealestate.com
Sun Estate Agent
0242 8361597
www.sunestate-tr.com
Taurean Properties
Tel 0252 6132377
www.taureanproperties.co.uk
Turyap
www.turyap.com.tr/english/
Xpress Homes
Tel 0242 8441281
www.kalkanapartments.com

ESTATE AGENTS
**East Mediterranean: Antalya,
Side, Alanya**
Arım Emlak
Tel 0242 887 2929
www.arimemlak.com

Let's Go To Turkey
Tel 0242 5132064
www.letsgototurkey.com
M&C Property
Tel 05322062928
www.mandcproperty.com
Properties in Turkey
Tel 0242 7536517
www.propertiesinturkey.com
Tolerance Realty
Tel 0242 5193056
www.tolerancerealty.com

ESTATE AGENTS
Istanbul
Aysen Real Estate
Tel 0212 2510409
Berkay Real Estate
Tel 0212 2929911
Istanbul Accommodation Centre
Tel 0212 292 89 44
www.istanbulaccommodationcentre.com
Mavi Ay Real Estate
Tel 0212 3252056
www.maviayestate.com
Sakir Real Estate Cihangir
Tel 0212 2939238
Eskidji Real Estate
Tel 0212 5322457
www.eskidji.com.tr
Remax
Tel 0212 2433333
www.remax.com.tr

FOREIGN CURRENCY DEALERS
Currencies Direct
Tel 020 78130332
www.currenciesdirect.com
HIFX
Tel 01753 859159
www.hifx.co.uk

HEALTHCARE
International Hospital (Istanbul)
Tel 0212 6633000
www.internationalhospital.com.tr

Eczacıbaş Sağlık Hizmetleri
Tel 0212 3172500
www.eczacibasi.com.tr
Esnaf Hstanesi (Fethiye)
Tel 0252 6126400
www.esnafhastanesi.com
Medicus Clinic (Side)
Tel 0242 753111
www.medicus.com.tr

INSURANCE
(Turkey)
Anadolu Sigorta
Tel 4440350
www.anadolusigorta.com.tr
AxaOyak
www.axaoyak.com.tr
Stewart International (title)
Tel 0212 284 7273
www.stewart.com

KITCHENS, FURNISHINGS
& ELECTRICAL
Arçelik
Tel 4440888
www.arcelik.com.tr
Beko
Tel 0212 2524900
www.beko.com.tr
Bellona
Tel 0800 361 89 86
www.bellona.com.tr
CK Yapı Dekorasyon
Custom-made kitchens country-wide. English-speaking staff.
Tel 0216 5419611
www.ckyapi.com.tr
Ipek Mobilya
Tel 0352 3220050
www.ipekmobilya.com.tr
Kelebek
Tel 0216 4467715
www.kelebek.com.tr
Mudo Concept Stores
Tel 0212 2852390
www.mudo.com.tr

LANGUAGE SCHOOLS
Dilmer
Tel 0212 2929696
www.dilmer.com
Tömer
Tel 0232 4640544
www.tomer.ankara.edu.tr/english/

OFFICIAL (UK)
Turkish Consulate (London)
Tel 020 7591 6900
www.turkishconsulate.org.uk
Turkish Embassy (Customs info)
Tel 020 72456318
Turkish Tourist Office (UK &
Ireland)
Tel 0207 629 7771
www.gototurkey.com

OFFICIAL (TURKEY)
Turkish Embassy
Tel 0312 4553344
www.britishembassy.org.tr
Ministry of Foreign Affairs (Visa information)
www.mfa.gov.tr/MFA/ConsularInformation/ForForeigners/
Turkish Touring & Automobile
Association
Tel 0212 2828140
www.turing.org.tr

PRIVATE MEDICAL INSURANCE
(see also: Insurance)
AXA PPP Healthcare
Tel 0800 121 345
www.axappphealthcare.co.uk
BUPA International
Tel 01273 208181
www.bupa-intl.com
ExpaCare Insurance Services
Tel 01344 381650
www.expacare.net

PROPERTY CONSULTANTS
Colliers Resco
Consultation and development services for investors. Tel 0212 2886262
www.colliers.com/Markets/Istanbu

PROPERTY MANAGEMENT
(see also: Estate Agents)
Alanya Answers
Tel 0242 5192138
www.alanya-answers.com
Windsor Property Management
Tel 0252 613 3585
www.alanya-answers.com

SOLICITORS
For a list of Turkish solicitors visit the Consular Services section of the British Embassy website:
www.britishembassy.org.tr
Acacia International
Tel 07000 56571 (UK)
www.acacia-int.com
Denton Wilde Sapte & Guner
Tel 0212 284 6091
www.dentonwildesapte.com

SWIMMING POOLS
Arites Inş aat
Tel 0216 3755000
www.arites.com.tr
Sistem Havuz
Tel 0242 2287958
www.sistemhavuz.com
Tekimsan
Tel 0216 471 8255
www.tekimsan.com.tr

TRANSPORT FIRMS
Crown Relocations (UK)
Tel 0113 385 1000
www.cronrelo.com
Robinsons International
Tel 01235 552266
www.robinsons-intl.com
Sumerman International Moving
Tel 0212 2235818
www.sumerman.com

UsefulWebsites

www.aegeanworld.com Aegean resorts information site
www.alanya.cc Alanya information
www.altinkum.com Altınkum information website
www.antalya-ws.com Antalya information site
www.bodrumlife.com Bodrum information portal
www.buyinginturkey.info A property information site where you can order this book
www.calis-beach.co.uk Çaliş information & forum
www.cornucopia.net Cornucopia magazine website
www.datcainfo.com Datça information
www.dalyan.co.uk Dalyan information
www.fethiye.net Fethiye information
www.gofethiye.com Fethiye information
www.gocek.info Göcek information website
www.ido.com.tr Online booking and times for Istanbul ferries
www.internationaleducationmedia.com/turkey a list of Turkish universities
www.kalkan.org.tr Kalkan local site
www.kilim.com buy a Turkish carpet online
www.kusadasi.net information site about the resort

www.letsgoturkey.com Turkey information site
www.marmaris.org Marmaris news and information
www.marmarisinfo.com Marmaris information site
www.mymerhaba.com Expat network & resource
www.oliveoilturkey.com website about Turkish olive oil
www.theguideturkey.com Guide to Istanbul, Antalya, Bodrum and other cities
www.timeout.com.tr Istanbul nightlife magazine
www.travelturkeymag.com Travel features and information
www.turkeytravelplanner.com Practical travel information
www.turkishculture.org Turkish Cultural site
www.turkishdailynews.com website of Turkey's English language newspaper.
www.turkey-news.com news about Turkey from the world's press
www.turkishpress.com News portal with Turkish & international news
www.turunc.com Turunç resort information
www.turkishwinetours.com Turkish wine-tasting tours

AdvertiserIndex

SPONSORED BY:
Alternative Travel
Currencies Direct
M&C Property